D0065819

Everyday Faith

Other books by Terry Pluto

Everyday Faith

Terry Pluto

Edited by Jan Leach

Gray & Company, Publishers • *Cleveland*

Psalm 68:6: God sets the lonely in families.

To my new God-given family: Mother Melva Hardison;
sisters Gloria Williams and Audrey Walker and Pat McCubbin.

I believe in the Biblical concept of tithing: ten percent of
everything I earn from this book will be donated to Akron's
Haven of Rest City Mission.

These columns and articles were originally published in the
Akron Beacon Journal

Gray & Company, Publishers · *Cleveland*
www.grayco.com

Library of Congress Cataloging-in-Publication Data
Pluto, Terry, 1955–
Everyday Faith / by Terry Pluto.
1. Christian life—United States. I. Title.
BV4510.3.P58 2004   248.4—dc22   2004000368

ISBN 1-886228-81-7
Printed in the United States of America
First printing

Contents

HOLIDAYS

Preface

The first time I really thought about The Life After was when I looked into the dying eyes of my father.

Those big blue eyes, blinking as they pleaded for help.

Wide, wet eyes.

Terrified eyes.

He was dying and he knew it. He didn't know when, but it wouldn't be long. He knew it and I knew it.

Until then, I believed in God, or at least something Bigger Than Us. And I figured there was a heaven, hell, or at least some place you go after it's all over.

But I ignored it, until it stared me in the eye, face-to-face with my father. Is there a God? If so, what does He mean to me? Does He have any claim on my life? Does He speak to us? Guide us? Or are we just supposed to blunder along and hope for the best?

I wrestled with those questions and more while spending nearly five years helping my father die from his stroke.

Maybe you have been eyeball-to-eyeball with death. It's looking down into the coffin of a grandmother, an infant, a friend. It's being in a near-fatal car wreck where someone else dies.

It's something that changes your life.

You're still here, but the other person is gone.

But where? And why? And what's the point?

My father's struggle with his stroke ended back in 1998. To be exact, it was Feb. 11, 1998, his 78th birthday.

I always found that strange, my father passing away exactly on his birthday.

Even more startling is that I was to be in Japan to cover the

Winter Olympics for the *Akron Beacon Journal*. I had a flight scheduled from Detroit to Tokyo. I was driving along the Ohio Turnpike, and I had this gnawing feeling not to get on that plane.

My father was in bad shape, but that had been the case for years. He had been in and out of the hospital six times over the previous six months.

As I was driving to the Detroit Airport, something told me not to go to Japan. I pulled into a truck stop outside of Toledo, called my bosses and told them that I wasn't sure I should go to the Olympics because of my father.

They told me to come home.

My father died 12 hours later, about when I would have been getting off the jet in Tokyo.

Did God speak to me?

My Christian friends believe so, and I do, too.

It wasn't a loud voice. It wasn't Paul being knocked to the ground and blinded by the light on the road to Damascus. It was just a feeling.

I tell you this because many people have had similar things happen to them. It's why there is a real hunger for God and things of God, even if we aren't sure who God is and what He wants from us.

This book is a collection of columns originally printed in the Your Faith section of the *Akron Beacon Journal*. I'm a sportswriter; I never thought I'd write columns about faith.

But after three years, I know these columns matter because readers have told me so.

I don't have a corner on morality. I sometimes dodge the "big issues." I try to write for people who are searching for God.

I don't spend time on abortion, gay bishops or church scandals. I do write about loneliness and temptation and whether prayer matters.

Those issues interest me, and I've discovered that many of you agree.

Before I started, several people in the media advised me to skip it.

"Writing about religion can kill your career," one friend said—and he is a person of faith.

But I don't write about religion.

I write that church is important, but God is bigger than any place of worship. I write from the perspective that there is an all-powerful God who created the universe, that the Holy Scriptures have value, and that God often speaks to us through them.

I don't have all the answers.

I just know my father was right when he insisted, "No one ever said life was fair."

At least not this life on earth.

Jesus once said, "You *will* have trouble in this world."

Psalm 23 reads, "*When* you walk through shadow of the valley of death . . ."

If you haven't been in those scary shadows, just wait.

I don't care if you are a Jew, a Christian, a Muslim or a skeptic; there is a spiritual thirst in most of us.

I try to write about God and us and what that means for our lives.

People have told me they are blessed by these stories, but believe me; it's the other way around.

For that, I'll always be grateful.

FAMILY

Dads: When Your Kids Look At You, They See God

Hey, dads, when your kids look at you, they see God.

Kind of scary, isn't it?

For many people, their first image of God comes from their father.

People who have trouble trusting God often had fathers who let them down, who lied to them. I've heard more than one story of children waiting for a divorced dad to show up on visitation day, only he didn't make it. Didn't even call.

Many of those people struggle with God, especially when they hear the prayer, "Our Father, who art in heaven . . ."

"If God is like my father, I better be careful and not expect much," they think.

There are some people who see God as The IRS Agent In The Sky just waiting for them to mess up. Their harsh, demanding, overly critical fathers often make them believe they can never please God. After a while, they tend to say, "Why even bother to try?"

People from families where the father was loving, where the father both disciplined and lifted them up tend to have a healthier image of God. When they read Paul saying in the Bible that we should call God "Abba," as in Daddy, they immediately embrace the idea.

There is a God in heaven who wants the best for them, a God who is not too busy to talk, a God who gives good advice through Scripture and other people of faith.

Then there are people whose fathers just disappeared. They sometimes see God as distant, too busy with the universe to care about them.

Don't think it's true?

Close your eyes and remember how you first saw God. Now, think of your father. Do they match?

For many, they do.

That's why Father's Day is so important.

This is not just a celebration of a man who made a commitment to support his wife and kids. It's so much more.

Sons look at their fathers to discover how a man acts. A father can talk to his children in a different way than a mother. And he can give his children the ultimate gift of loving and supporting their mother, modeling what it means to be a father, a husband and a man.

Daughters often use their fathers as a way to gauge how a man (and a possible future husband) should treat them. Does he listen to Mom? Does he sell out his family for a promotion? Does he use the silent treatment when angry? Does he get physical? Or does he sit down and try to talk things out?

Bottom line: Fathers matter.

Ask anyone who grew up without one. Or with a lousy one. Or a drunken, addicted, violent one. Or with a dad who made them feel loved, who cared about them enough to set limits and insist that the basic rules of civilized behavior be followed.

It's true that not every person with a Father Problem has a God Problem or Life Problem. There are heroic mothers and grandmothers who modeled God's compassion, whose determination, self-sacrifice and prayers kept their children on the proper path.

Often, a grandfather, uncle or some other Father Figure steps up to help that single mom with the child.

But the facts are that children from fatherless homes are at least twice as likely to drop out of school, become pregnant in high school and end up in prison.

I repeat: Fathers matter.

That may seem obvious, but there is a growing trend in society that says otherwise.

A story by syndicated columnist Linda Chavez mentioned a government-funded study by Child Trends that asked the question, "Do you agree that one parent can bring up a child as well as two parents together?"

Forty-two percent of women agreed with that; only 26 percent of men did.

That makes no sense.

Sure, a single mom can bring up a good kid. But wouldn't it be easier and better if two committed parents shared the job?

Among minorities, 64 percent agreed that one parent is enough, which Child Trends says matches the birthrate of single parents in that community.

It seems that a large portion of women have lost confidence in the ability of men to be honorable fathers. And maybe that's because so many men have grown up without fathers in the home, so they don't know how they are supposed to act.

It's not going to change unless we say, "Hey, we've got a Father Problem here, we better start training our men in schools and churches." Older men who have been decent fathers have to start teaching the young men about fatherhood.

I once talked to a guy who was in solitary confinement in an area jail. He was about 18 and had been busted on drug charges. He also had a child.

"I'm just hurting myself," he said.

"But you're not there for your son," I said.

"I know," he said. "But I grew up without a dad, and I came out OK."

He was serious.

And so is the problem.

Pretending it's not is just asking for more trouble, more kids who are looking to Dad for everything from spiritual to practical guidance—only to have their hearts broken because no one is there.

Saturday, June 14, 2003

Keep Them In Church to Keep Them Out of Trouble

It's about 11 p.m. You're walking down a lonely street. Suddenly, several teen-age boys appear, laughing and dressed like most teen-agers, which means they have some part of their body pierced and their pants hang a little low.

Maybe you get a little nervous.

Then you notice something in their hands. Each is carrying a Bible. You overhear that they just came from a church youth group.

Do you feel relieved?

According to research from the University of North Carolina, you should.

From 1996 to 2000, that university conducted a massive study of teen-agers between the ages of 13 and 17.

The conclusion?

The more church services high school students attended, the more church groups they were involved with, the more religious study they did, the less likely they were to get in trouble.

Now that doesn't mean every church kid is a saint or every kid who skips church is ready to create hell on earth.

But the point of this National Study of Youth & Religion is that faith matters. Faith makes most of us, especially teen-agers, better people. Faith usually means the kids come from more stable families.

This isn't just an opinion; it's research based on 2,478 cases.

The report reveals: "Religious 12th-graders are less likely to drink and more likely to postpone their first time getting drunk.

When they do drink, they are less likely to get drunk as compared to non-religious 12th-graders."

On and on it goes.

They are less likely to use drugs, less likely to engage in crime and violence, more likely to be involved in sports, student government and other after-school activities. They usually have better relationships with their parents and are more likely to volunteer for community projects.

Interestingly, students who are the most active in church are the least likely to have been even offered drugs.

The research revealed that one in seven high school seniors admitted having sold drugs in the previous year. But only 7 percent of regular church-attenders did so, compared with 21 percent of non-attenders.

And the study showed that 38 percent of regular church-goers used some type of illegal drug (mostly marijuana) in the last year, compared with 61 percent of non-attenders.

Most of us don't need this 65-page glossy report to tell us the obvious: A real faith supplies direction and values, and kids need direction and values.

But it is nice that Christian Smith and his crew from the University of North Carolina made a significant study of this issue, especially in an age when there are so many voices in society claiming faith doesn't matter.

Here's the disclaimer: There are frauds and hypocrites in every religious setting, and some awful acts of violence have been carried out in the name of God.

But we are talking about getting the odds on our side.

Ask yourself this: "Have you ever heard anyone say they followed the Ten Commandments and it destroyed their life?"

We live in a world where some people don't know where they came from, why they are here, or where they are going. Those are three of life's big questions, and when they are unanswered, the world can be a very scary place.

People who don't care about what happens to them probably won't care about what happens to you. And they may decide life isn't worth living—for them, or us.

Think about the school shootings, the hideous crimes and the incredible self-destructive behavior carried out by some teen-agers. Think of the teen suicide rate. Think of how so many teen-agers seem angry, lost and depressed.

"About 95 percent of the kids here come from broken families and virtually no religious background, other than they may have a praying grandmother," said Tim Smith, superintendent of Summit County's juvenile detention facility on Dan Street in Akron.

Many of Smith's young people come from poverty and families ravaged by drugs.

But even "good kids"—from homes where all the basic needs are met and there is plenty of extra cash and goodies to go around—are looking for something they can believe in, something more than getting a good job, a nice house and a healthy paycheck.

A number of young people who have cars and parents get in trouble, too.

Why?

It's not about stuff.

It's about faith.

It's about believing in a God who tells us how to live.

Some people will use the National Study of Youth & Religion as a vehicle to promote school prayer, but the real question isn't whether we pray in school.

It's whether we pray at home.

The home is the first church. The home is the first place kids get their image of God. The home is where faith and values must be taught.

A father who drops mom and the kids off at church gives the message, especially to his sons, that this is just for women and children. The parent who uses the church youth group as a baby-sitter service, but never prays with the kids at home or takes them to services on the weekends undermines all the work of churches.

The key part of the study revealed that young people who say faith is "very important" and who "regularly attend" religious activities are more likely to live productive lives.

And, usually, they learned that at home.

Saturday, September 28, 2002

You Don't Hear Much in Church About Getting Along With Your Siblings

Have you ever heard a sermon about how to get along with your brothers and sisters?

Not the ones in your church or temple.

The real ones.

The brother who bullied you, who told you that you were stupid.

The sister your dad loved best.

The brothers and sisters who saw you at your worst.

"It's a wonderful topic," said the Rev. Joseph Kraker from St. Vincent's Church, "and I'd talk about it if I knew what to say."

Ain't it the truth?

Sometimes, it's so hard to know what to tell someone who grew up in the same house with you, someone who shared the same parents. And, maybe, someone who is so different from you.

A friend recently said: "I get along great with my brother. We're careful never to talk about anything important."

Not a bad strategy—at least for some families.

"I've had problems with people in my own family," Kraker admitted. "I bet most of us have, and that's why we do need to talk about it."

But we often don't.

"I know I've never (preached) on it," said the Rev. David Klein from the Church of New Hope Assembly of God in Stow.

He added: "About half of the weddings and funerals I do

have siblings who aren't talking to each other, haven't been doing it for years."

Another friend talked about hiring an off-duty policeman to make sure the family stayed civil during Uncle Joe's funeral.

Maybe that's an extreme case, but just talk to people who have been through an estate settlement. Old grudges don't just surface, they boil over and threaten to blow up the room and splinter families.

"We talk a lot about forgiveness in the church," Klein said. "But that's often hardest in our own families. The Bible tells us to be our brother's keeper."

That comes from Genesis, Chapter 4.

The first children in the Bible are Cain and Abel. Cain believes that God likes Abel best, so he kills Abel.

God tells Cain that He favored Abel because Abel gave his best offerings to God. Cain just passed on the leftovers. Rather than shape up, Cain takes his brother's life, murdering him in a field.

"Where's your brother, Abel?" God asks Cain.

"I don't know," Cain replies. "Am I my brother's keeper?"

Most of us have done that in our own family. A parent wants to know about a brother or sister, and we say, "Not my department."

Our attitude is, we have enough of our own problems.

"We may not actually kill our siblings, but we can destroy them with what we say," Klein said. "It is hard to find a family where there isn't something going on."

The Chapel's Knute Larson is another pastor who said he's intrigued by the topic, but has never delivered a message just on sibling relationships.

"We teach on love and returning good for evil, but that's often hardest to do in your own home," he said.

Larson often jokes about his brother in his sermons. He talks about some friends who have brothers or sisters who are "best friends."

He said he sees his brother a few times a year, "and it's good, but we're not extremely close."

That goes for most siblings.

And most, when they take time to think about it, wish it were better.

Pastor Randy Baker did talk to his Akron Bible Church about the subject.

"For years, my sister prayed for me to get saved," he said. "But she was smart. She was patient and just loved the hell out of me.

"So many times, we pray for a brother or sister to change, but we don't pray for our attitude towards them to change."

That's just as hard as them changing.

"You can't fool your brother or sister," Baker said. "They know things about you that no one else does."

We may see a sibling with a great job who is very popular, and we remember when he was just an arrogant jerk as a kid. Or how she manipulated everyone in the family to get what she wanted, and she's probably still doing the same thing.

"Because we have the same genetics, we often expect our brothers and sisters to act and think just like us," said Dave Scavuzzo, pastor of Northampton United Methodist Church.

And there's something else.

"When it comes to our families, we can be kind of arrogant and think that the world would just be a better place if everybody acted like me," Scavuzzo added. "But I have nine brothers and sisters, and my mother has said she wished she had a couple more just to see how different they'd come out—and we really are so different."

Rabbi David Lipper of Temple Israel said envy and money often are behind the problems.

"And these things can be passed from generation to generation," Lipper said.

That's why it's important to address them.

"The most successful family doesn't compete and doesn't feel threatened by each other," Lipper said. "It's funny—we'll compromise in other areas of our life to get along, but it's tougher in our own families."

Lipper said we need to reach back to that special tie you have with your siblings, something that only you have.

"The natural tendency in families is for us to spread our wings and show our independence," he said.

But, sometimes, what we really need to do, is try to open our arms and give—even if it hurts a little bit.

Saturday, June 1, 2002

When Sons Follow Their Fathers' Footsteps Into Trouble

Fathers & Sons.

Harry Watson is a chaplain at the Summit County jail, where he has seen some heartbreaking father/son reunions.

Behind bars.

Wearing orange jumpsuits and shower slippers.

Staring at their hands, wondering where it all went wrong.

Sometimes, they hadn't seen each other for a decade, yet they end up incarcerated for the same type of crimes.

Fathers & Sons.

The *Beacon Journal* recently ran four days of stories about sons who murdered their fathers—the tragic result of years of neglect, abuse and violence.

Those are the most extreme cases, but there are millions of others nearly as damaging.

Former Browns defensive-end-turned-prison-evangelist Bill Glass often says, "Not everyone with a father problem ends up in prison, but virtually everyone in prison has a father problem."

Glass says inmates are given free access to Mother's Day cards and Father's Day cards.

"They usually run out of the cards for the mothers," he said. "The fathers' cards just sit there. You can walk up and down death row and find men who love their mothers, but hate their fathers."

Fathers & Sons.

"I think of pictures of little boys wearing their father's big hat and shoes," said Watson. "But when that father is an alcoholic or a drug addict, so many times that happens to the son. I have seen it over and over in jail."

Broken men sit there, fighting back the tears, talking about how they saw their fathers shoot up dope. Or how they saw their fathers get drunk, then smack around mom and the kids.

And how they promised themselves that they wouldn't end up like their fathers—but they did. It's the old line about "the apple doesn't fall far from the tree."

The Bible talks about "sins of the fathers" visited upon the next generations. Several polls have indicated that the best indicator of someone going to jail is if the father had also served time.

At Akron's Haven of Rest Rescue Mission, Chaplain Gary Meeks sees it.

"We've had one family where four brothers passed through here," he said. "You'll talk to a guy and he'll tell you that he had a 'normal' family. He said his father worked, was married to mom. That sounds good . . ."

Until the man later talks about the extreme beatings the father gave the children. Or how he ran the streets, and mom never knew when (or if) he'd come home.

"To them, it's normal, because it's all they know," Meeks said. "But when they get older, they know something was wrong with that, and something is very wrong in their lives."

Fathers & Sons.

"A lot of men can't forgive their fathers for what happened when they were growing up," said Curt Thomas III, the director of the men's division at the Haven of Rest.

That's why you see so many men who are angry, men who are withdrawn, men who don't know how to be men.

"I've heard it said the greatest gift a man can give his children is to love their mother," said Meeks. "Most of the troubled men are from families where the mother wasn't loved by her husband, and these guys don't know how to love their wives."

And there is chaos and bitterness in the home.

"Sometimes, when there is a father who is very mean, the child starts to wonder if something is wrong with him," Meeks said. "That he deserved the beatings."

And a father who loves his wife and cares for his family, tends to produce sons who do the same.

Certainly some sons have overcome the absence of a father, or a father whose behavior left a lot to be desired. But they will tell you that it was hard, that they had to find other male role models.

"A relationship with God really helps," Meeks said. "Your heavenly father can be the father you've never had. And I've seen that make a difference in the lives of a lot of men."

Saturday, May 12, 2001

A Valentine Husbands Can Give Throughout the Year

OK, guys, listen up.

I write that because we're not very good at . . . listening.

At least not when our wives are trying to talk to us.

I plead guilty to this charge. I'll insist I'm much better than I used to be, but I still need work.

I'm capable of giving undivided attention to someone in a business setting. When I interview someone, my goal is to make him or her feel like the most important person in the world, like I can't wait to hear the next word that comes from his or her lips.

At home?

Well, sometimes I sort of grunt when Roberta is telling me something.

Or I cut her off in mid-sentence and tell her *exactly* what she needs to do, and it's time to stop talking and get to work.

Charming, don't you think?

There is a Jewish proverb about loneliness eating up the soul.

Most of us can identify with that, but most men forget that women sometimes want us to shut off the ball game, put away the newspaper, turn on the answering machine and ignore the phone.

You probably wonder who died and set me up as a marriage expert.

No one.

I just know that I nearly emotionally killed my wife early in our 25-year marriage because I was so driven, so wrapped up in my career, so determined to impress everyone.

Except her.

Things are much better between us.

But I do regret those times when she'd be in the middle of telling me something I considered trivial, and I'd say, "OK," . . . and pick up the phone to call someone . . . before she even finished.

Now, I realize how that had hurt her, made her feel insignificant.

Psalm 46:10 tells us, "Be still and know I am God." It's also not a bad strategy to use with the women in our lives.

Be still and listen.

Be still and don't try to fix her.

Be still, but look her in the eye.

Ask questions that indicate you are paying attention, instead of making snide comments intended to make her feel stupid or irrelevant. Then encourage her. Tell her that she matters to you and to God. If she asks for your advice, give it.

If not, try this.

Take her hands and pray with her about the problem. Ask God to intervene in the situation at work, with her family, with the kids, whatever is on her mind.

Ask her to pray.

And be still.

The book of Romans tells us, "Be devoted to one another, love one another, honor one another above ourselves."

Maybe that's easy for you, but it can be a massive task for me.

I remember when I began to pray with my wife. I felt dumb. I didn't exactly know what to say. I finally imagined God being in the room with us. I prayed for wisdom for her, for comfort, for strength.

I reminded myself that, like God, she doesn't grade on style points, just on the condition of my heart. And now I can say that prayer has helped cement our marriage.

I'm writing this because I recently read an article called "Why Women Leave Men," by Dr. Willard Harley, author of a fine book called *His Needs, Her Needs*.

Harley's research revealed that women are *twice* as likely as men to file for divorce, and the main reason isn't drugs, alcohol, physical abuse or adultery.

It's "mental cruelty," which basically means "husbands being indifferent, failing to communicate . . . emotional abandonment."

This shocked me.

Bringing home a decent paycheck, staying loyal to her and providing a nice home isn't enough. Women say they want more than things from us: They want *us*.

Obviously, there are exceptions. Some women are hung up on status. Others are destined to be unhappy, no matter who their husband is.

But this issue of communication, of them wanting to talk to us about their lives and wanting to hear what is happening with us, is serious business to women.

One of the biggest lies rammed down our throats is that men and women are alike. They don't look the same. They don't think the same. They don't talk the same. Psalm 139 speaks of each of us being "fearfully and wonderfully made."

So it's a waste of time for a man to say, "If I were her, I would . . ."

She is different, period. As guys, we need to remember that.

Saturday, February 15, 2003

Have Youth Sports Become Too Important?

This is a story in which faith and sports mix.

It's also a story that will make some youth coaches very unhappy. That's a shame, because most coaches are excellent people who are incredibly underpaid and overburdened for the jobs they do.

But sometimes, they lose perspective.

Like when they schedule practices on Christmas Day. A few youth coaches did just that.

Why?

As several ministers said, "Why divide families like this? Why make parents have to decide between church and practice? Or between a family gathering and pleasing a coach?"

Why have youth sports become so important?

One coach said he needed the time on the court because his team would soon be traveling to a holiday tournament.

So what?

If his team wasn't already prepared, another day of practice wasn't going to make much difference. But pro and college coaches usually practice nearly every day, and so do some coaches at lower levels.

A coach may say, "Hey, it's just a couple of hours. You can visit with family after."

Actually, it's four hours. A kid has to leave an hour before practice, and usually it takes an hour after practice for him to shower up and return home. It disrupts what should be a day strictly for family and worship.

It's not just Christmas. It's Easter. It's the Fourth of July. And, yes, it's Sunday mornings.

A friend told me, "My 10-year-old daughter was invited to play in a soccer league, but the games were on Sunday, starting at noon."

My friend's church services begin at 11 a.m. and often don't end until 12:30 p.m.

His daughter wants to play. He wants the entire family in church. Guess who looks like the bad guy.

Bud Olszewski is the Rittman High School boys soccer coach. He also is pastor of Grace Brethren Church in Rittman.

"As far as I know, no teams in our community practiced on Christmas," he said. "My soccer season is in the fall, and I don't even like the practice on Labor Day. I hate the idea of taking away time from family and their kids."

But Olszewski admitted there was a holiday "about five years ago" when he had a "voluntary practice."

In this case, there was no penalty if a kid failed to show up. But generally when coaches have "optional" practices, the message is clear: Be there. Especially if you're not a star and you're competing for playing time.

Olszewski speaks as both a coach and a pastor. He was surprised to hear about Christmas practices, and the coach in him said, "Sometimes, it's a good idea for kids to have a day off just to let their young bodies recover."

The pastor in him wondered about the message this sends, how sports has become a god for so many families.

For decades, the National Football League has been high church for some people, and you have to wonder what kids learn when they see some of their parents slamming down the beers at 10 on a Sunday morning, tailgating in a stadium parking lot, awaiting a big game.

Glory to God, and pass the communion of brats and Budweiser.

Older priests and pastors are astounded at how America moved from a country that didn't even sell gasoline on Sundays to one where everything is open, 24/7.

That's 24 hours a day, seven days a week.

No time to stop. No time to spend a morning in God's presence, or even just have a long breakfast and play with the kids.

In some families, church is shoehorned in between games and practices. Over and over, you hear that teams have to play/practice on Sunday mornings because, "that's the only time the field/gym/ice is open."

So what then is most important—church, family or sports?

"I know the answer to that question, and it hurts," said the Rev. Joe Kraker of St. Vincent Catholic Church in Akron. "Some families don't even sit down and have a meal together. You see some of these moms driving from one sport to another, one game to another. They're never home."

Kraker said the Catholic Youth Organization sports teams don't start Sunday games until 1 p.m., so families can attend church.

"But you see so many families running in so many different directions, and it should be no surprise that some families are falling apart," Kraker said.

And it's time for families and coaches both to stop and think about that.

Saturday, January 6, 2001

Ever have someone in your family who is a prodigal?

That's the brother/sister who spent his/her life creating a massive family mess, wearing everyone out, doing exactly what he/she pleased and not caring what anyone else thought.

Then the prodigal comes home, and the parents are so happy.

Suppose you have been the good sister/brother. Not perfect, but you usually try to do the right thing. You're the one they call when someone is sick, someone needs a ride, something needs fixing.

And you go.

Maybe not always with a smile, but you go.

A sense of serving lives in your heart.

So does a little resentment because the prodigal has demanded so much attention, caused so much grief, cost so much money. Part of you feels as if you've been taken for granted. You know that's not an admirable reaction, but it's honest.

That's why I've always been sympathetic to the older brother in the parable of the prodigal son, which Jesus tells in Luke, Chapter 15.

Most of it deals with the selfish knucklehead of a younger son who grabs his inheritance early, runs from the family and blows his cash. He ends up broke, working in a pigpen.

He comes home truly sorry, begging for nothing more than to be a servant to his father. He isn't arrogant. He doesn't expect to be treated like a son. He is willing to start over, pay dues, try to rebuild bridges to the family.

(Too bad some of us who've dealt with our own prodigals didn't see them return with the same humility. Most often, it's with an annoying sense of entitlement.)

The father welcomes the kid brother with a hug, an expensive robe and a joyous party featuring the prime steaks "because this son of mine was lost and now he is found," proclaims the father.

The older son is angry.

He wonders why he never had a party like this, why his father is so excited about a brother who has done so little for the family. So the older brother refuses to go to the party, indulging in a little self-pity and a minor-league hissy fit.

Ever been there?

When this parable is preached, it's often about God's desire for sinners to come home. And many times, the older brother is dismissed as self-righteous and unforgiving.

If that's the case, I plead guilty.

Not so much because of an immediate-family situation, but because it has happened at work and other social settings. People who have been consistently lazy and irresponsible shape up for five minutes, and suddenly some act as if they are candidates for sainthood.

That is hard for some of us to take.

That was the case with the older brother when he boycotted the family.

His father invites him in, but the brother says, "All these years I've been slaving for you and never disobeyed your orders. Yet you never even gave me a young goat so I could celebrate with my friends. But when this son of yours who has squandered your money with prostitutes comes home, you kill the fatted calf for him."

Actually, we don't know that the kid brother was hanging

out with hookers—the older brother just says he did. He also forgets that the oldest son has an exalted status in Jewish tradition, so he probably had a very good deal at home and no doubt ate very well.

But the older brother thinks, "They always loved *him* best." Haven't many of us felt like that?

That's why I love the end of the parable, the part that is so often ignored from the pulpit.

The father is wise. He knows the heart of his son, feels the pain.

The father says, "You are always with me, and everything I have is yours. But we had to celebrate and be glad, because this brother of yours was dead and is alive again; he was lost and is found."

We don't know whether the older son went to the party, because Jesus ended the parable with the father's words.

But I believe the older brother followed his father, because he always had before. I sense the older brother just needed to be reassured, to know the father appreciates his loyalty.

So often, people who are like the older brother—be it in families, in worship centers or on the job—can easily be ignored. They need to know they matter. They need to know someone is watching, be it the father, mother, boss, coach.

The father tells him, "Everything I have is yours."

He's saying the payoff is coming, I do love you, now let's go in and love your brother a little bit.

When we hear those words from someone we respect and love, it's so much easier for us to love someone who, right now, might not be the most lovable person to us.

Saturday, May 3, 2003

VALUES

Bald-Headed Lies

A pastor wore a hairpiece for 20 years. On a recent Sunday, he took it off during a sermon to make a point about pride and the masks we wear.

The folks in the pews gasped, as if the man had suddenly appeared at the pulpit buck naked. But many found their pastor more human, and attendance at his church soared.

Being follicularly challenged, I can identify with the bald preacher.

I never went for a wig, hair transplants or even Rogaine. But for about 15 years, I wore my hair very long on the sides and back—as if that somehow made up for what was missing on top. I had the grungy look of a guy who spent an inordinate amount of time sleeping outside while not on familiar terms with a razor.

Then I realized: I'm bald!

That wasn't exactly a bulletin to my friends, who had noticed the diminishing returns on my head for decades. But I never wanted to cut my hair short because I'd look like my father. At 40, I finally decided there could be worse things than being a middle-aged bald guy.

All of which made me think of the silly things that we carry around.

A friend told me about a van that he's been trying to sell for months. He listed it at $4,900, and he had to get at least $4,000 for it. Exactly why it *had* to be $4,000 is unclear, other than he's certain that's what the van is worth.

Part of his own value became tangled up with the quest to sell for his price. In the meantime, he's paying insurance on it, and the frustrations of seeing people back out of offers have been mounting. He knows he's spending far too much time thinking about a van that he didn't even want anymore.

"The other day, I was wondering if I should just give the van away," he said. "Take the (tax) write-off and be rid of it."

Sounds like a plan with potential.

But isn't it hard just to get rid of all the extra stuff?

And isn't it easy for most of us to decide we're underpaid, overworked and not appreciated?

Give me 10 minutes, a few basic facts about your situation, and I bet I can convince you that you're getting a raw deal. And I'm sure you can do the same for me.

Isn't there someone at your workplace with a better office, a prime parking spot that he never really earned? Shouldn't you have a parking spot, too? Or how about a better title? And certainly, a raise is in order.

Why doesn't your husband understand what it's like to be home with the kids, trying to clean house and driving them all over creation for games and lessons? Why does he think he's the only one who ever gets tired?

If you don't feel that way now, don't worry: you will.

Professional sports executives hate it when *USA Today* runs its listing of all athletes' salaries. If the players don't bother to study it, the girlfriends/wives/parents do. They find someone who is making more than the man they love.

"Look, honey, Player X is making $9 million, and you're only getting $7 million this year," a wife will say. "They're cheating you, because you're twice as good as that guy!"

At $7 million or $9 million a year? After taxes and the agent's cut, what's the difference? It's an obscene amount of money for playing a kid's game, yet it's hard not to measure ourselves by our paychecks.

Or our positions at work.

Or our popularity with friends.

Or as comedian Tommy Smothers used to tell brother Dick every week on TV, "Mom always liked you best!"

Isn't there someone in our family who loves someone more than us, and we can't figure out why?

I love the Book of Proverbs. Reading through Chapter 16, we're told:

How much better to get wisdom than gold, to choose understanding rather than silver.

But the rage of Wall Street executives and high-powered salesmen is Botox, the treatment that is supposed to take away wrinkles—especially those lines in your forehead that reveal your mood. A recent study of the American Society of Plastic Surgeons discovered that 12 percent of patients wanted to get rid of "angry/severe facial expressions." They think it will help them make favorable deals because the person across the bargaining table won't be able to guess what they're thinking by reading their face.

And it makes them look younger, too!

Plastic surgery.

Hair coloring.

Nails that appeared to have been painted by Picasso and cost nearly as much as a piece of art by one of the grand masters.

Proverbs says: Gray hair is a crown of splendor; it's attained by a righteous life.

Hard to believe, unless you happen to be like me—with no hair at all.

Meanwhile, we fill our lives with things we don't need to impress people we don't even like.

Haven't all of us been there?

Proverbs says: A heart at peace gives life to the body, but envy rots the bones.

We like to believe we don't fall for all those bald-faced lies that lead us to cover up some frailty or insecurity. But down deep, don't most of us know we're really trying to hide something? And isn't it time we just took a chance and exposed ourselves as who we really are, even if it's being a bald guy or someone who has a van no one else wants? Aren't there worse things in life?

Saturday, August 3, 2002

Those Who May Not Believe in God Stand Up for Those Who Do

The best thing to come out of the Pledge of Allegiance ruling by Judge Alfred Goodwin is that people who may not even believe in God decided to stand up for those who do.

Name another issue that has so united the country as Goodwin stating that part of the pledge is unconstitutional because of the phrase "under God."

The judge has since issued a delay of his own ruling, awaiting more legal action. In the meantime, he ought to travel to Afghanistan, where the bombs are still falling, the mines exploding, the blood being spilled.

CNN reported U.S. troops were "bewildered" by the decision.

Not as much as the judge himself must have been when he wrote the ruling.

Wouldn't it be great if the suit filed by Dr. Michael Newdow on behalf of his second-grade daughter reaches the U.S. Supreme Court? And before the arguments begin, the court's marshal says, "God save this honorable court"?

That's right, before each U.S. Supreme Court session, the marshal says, "God save this honorable court."

And for the record, your honor, that hasn't exactly stopped the Supreme Court from churning out some decisions that people of faith would consider very hostile.

The man who brought the suit is a physician in Sacramento. He also has a law degree. He says he did it because, "I'm an atheist and this offends me."

Suppose someone is a communist, anarchist or a royalist.

Suppose parts of the pledge dealing with our form of government offended them? Should the courts decide that the parts about "liberty" and "justice" be eliminated?

If you don't like the pledge, or don't agree with the pledge— just keep quiet.

You have the right to do that. The U.S. Supreme Court ruled as much in 1943, in a case brought by the Jehovah's Witnesses, who objected to part of the pledge. In essence, the court said the pledge can be said in public, but participation is optional. Nor is anyone compelled to salute the flag.

But it's not enough for Newdow, who said his quest began when he stared at a coin and saw the phrase: In God We Trust.

He said, "I don't trust in God," and began plotting lawsuits.

Doesn't he have anything better to do? And why drag your second-grade daughter into the debate to advance your political agenda? He admitted to CNN that his daughter has not received any harassment from teachers or other students.

"My daughter is in the lawsuit because you need that for standing," he admitted.

Bet she'll like hearing that when she grows up and realizes how she was used, especially since it's not for the first time. Her father filed a similar suit in Florida, but that one was dismissed. That was in 1998, when the girl was five.

Dr. Newdow told reporters he quit his job as an emergency room doctor to "fight the government" on this issue, and has represented himself, claiming to have spent 4,000 hours on the cause.

He also said he's upset about government shoving "God down my throat."

Well, he has every right to keep his mouth shut.

Some people wince when they hear God's name used in certain ways. Yet no one is suing to keep divine-based profanity out of public discussion, otherwise 90 percent of Hollywood's movies would be banned.

The ruling came from a three-judge panel headed by Goodwin on the 9th U.S. Circuit Court of Appeals. This court's decisions have been overruled in 12 of 16 cases this year. In 1997, it was 28 of 29. If most of us had that track record, we'd be looking for a job, not trying to rewrite the Pledge of Allegiance.

The judges pointed out that the phrase "under God" was added to the pledge in 1954 by Congress and President Eisenhower. The pledge had been written in 1892, and evolved over the last century.

Goodwin's majority opinion stated the pledge has a "coercive effect on young children."

On what planet?

Even Dr. Newdow didn't claim that was the case for his daughter.

This isn't about prayer in schools, or about setting up a government based on a certain religion. It's what happens when the courts take freedom *of* religion, and try to transform it into freedom *from* religion—a huge difference.

How about someone filing a lawsuit to bring back common sense?

For that, turn to the dissenting decision of Judge Ferdinand Fernandez. He wrote that the pledge didn't bother anyone, "except the fevered eye of persons who fervently would like to drive all tincture of religion out of public life."

When does a war on religion become a religion in itself? Maybe the courts ought to consider that question.

Saturday, June 29, 2002

It's Not Easy to Treat Our Neighbors as We Would Like to be Treated

"It's Hard to Serve God."

That's the title of a sermon I'd like to hear.

It is hard to serve God. We need to admit it, talk about it and support each other as we try to do it.

I'm not talking about volunteering somewhere or helping out at a school or place of worship.

It's more like taking the advice of Jesus, who said, "Love God with all your heart, and love your neighbor as yourself."

I blow it every day.

I'm telling you this because in every church, temple or mosque, there are people who seem to make living God's way seem so easy.

And they make the rest of us feel so guilty.

Some of them are just self-righteous phonies, but others are genuinely good people, in tune with God. They have come to a peaceful understanding of how to live and seem to know what God wants from them.

But most of us probably struggle in this area.

We can say: I don't do heavy drugs, I don't get stinking drunk, I don't beat my spouse, I don't grab a gun and hold up the Dairy Queen when my wallet is a little light.

But we know God isn't just talking about that.

It's about treating everyone as we'd want to be treated.

Sounds good, but just try it.

There are times when I don't think much of some of the people in my life, times when I don't want to be kind or patient, times when I act like a jerk.

Even worse, I'll be in the middle of acting like a jerk . . . and I'll know I'm acting like a jerk . . . and I'll keep doing it anyway.

Several of the Ten Commandments can be summed up like this: Thou shall not act like a jerk.

Or how about this: Thou shall not be grumpy.

Or needy.

Or petty.

I like to think of myself as an honest person. . . .

But I have to be honest: I'm not.

At least not all the time.

I catch myself telling self-serving little lies. When I'm 15 minutes late, I'll sometimes start to blame the traffic. Hey, everyone can understand that, right? And I did sit at the red light for a while . . . at least a minute or two.

The real problem was I messed around at home, got a late start, and it was all my fault.

And I hate to admit it.

Then there's this habit that I've finally started to break.

I'd tell my boss that I spent 45 minutes interviewing someone, when it was more like 20 minutes.

My boss didn't care—45 or 20 minutes, so what? He just wanted the story.

But I wanted him to know I really worked, I got all this time with this important person, and he should appreciate me.

I lied.

Or what about this?

Most of us want to be liked. People ask us for a favor. We don't want to do it, and we don't know if we can do it.

What do we do?

Too many times, we say we'll do it—or at least we'll try—because we don't want to disappoint them. We don't want to look bad in their eyes.

What happens?

Too often, we don't come through, which alienates the people who asked.

Or if we do the favor, we sometimes have a crummy attitude and are very resentful, which is not much better than not doing it at all.

As a sportswriter, I associate with athletes who spend time watching game films. Their actions are critiqued, slowed-down and played over and over, just to make a point.

How would any of us like to watch the video of our life over any given 24 hours? Or listen to tapes of some phone conversations? Or look at still photos of some of our worst facial expressions? The rolling of our eyes to put someone down without uttering a sound is not a glossy photo we'd like to have framed and hung on the wall.

I'm not writing this to make anyone feel lousy.

Rather, it's to have us all admit we have some problems.

Still don't think so?

How about gossip?

Not just telling it, but listening to it.

Someone says, "Did you hear about Mrs. X, and *why* her husband really filed for divorce?"

Don't tell me that it's simple to walk away from that conversation.

According to God's word, being an audience for gossip is just as bad as spreading it. That's partly because it's nearly impossible not to tell someone else when we've heard something especially juicy.

Here's another tough one: coveting, which is mentioned in two different commandments.

That means being jealous because someone has something we want, or being jealous because someone got the promotion or attention we wanted.

It can be as basic as saying, "Mom always loved you best."

Sound difficult to live this way?

That's because it is, and we need to help each other, which is a message that should be shouted from every pulpit.

Saturday, April 5, 2003

What Happened to God's Day?

I need both hands and most of my fingers to count all the commandments that I've broken. Hey, I never killed anyone, but there have been days when I've given it serious thought.

Bet you have, too.

But there is one commandment that I break more than any other, and I never even realized it until recently.

It's No. 4 on God's Top 10: "Thou shall keep holy God's Day. Six days you shall work and accomplish all your work, but the seventh day is a Sabbath to the Lord, and you shall not do any work."

If you take time to consider it, this is much bigger than going to your temple, mosque or church. It's about making time for God, for family, even for yourself.

It's shutting down for a day.

How many of us do that?

In the fall, I slip church into the mornings of the Browns games that I'm supposed to cover for the *Akron Beacon Journal*. Those Sundays often end up as some of my longest work days.

So I try to pick a day in the middle of the week. This will be my day of rest. A day to read, to pray, to talk to friends. After a few hours, I'm ready to do something. Or, at least, I feel like I should be doing something.

As Pastor David Loar of Fairlawn-West United Church of Christ said, "Far more of us are addicted to work than to drugs, alcohol or anything else. We stop for a while, and our body craves action. We start to fidget. We think of everything we could be doing."

Guilty.

We hear the phrase "24/7," as in 24 hours a day, seven days a week. Always open. I remember thinking it was ridiculous that some of the Kinko's stores were open every day, every hour, every minute of the year.

Then I found myself at one making copies at about 2 a.m.

I thought, "This is crazy."

So are most of our lives.

I have e-mail. I have three phones in my house. I have answering machines at home and at the office. I have a cell phone that usually is hanging from my belt when I'm away from the phones at home.

I am wired.

I bet a lot of you are, too.

"Worship is supposed to be at the center of the Sabbath Day," said the Rev. Gordon Yahner of St. Hilary's in Fairlawn. "God gives us the gift of time, and we should give it back to him."

Some people have said, "Those religious types just say that because they want you to go to their churches and give money. I can get closer to God by going for a long walk in the woods, or just sitting outside and reading than I can in church."

Maybe so.

But how many of us do that?

How often do we take that long walk in the woods? How often do we spend that morning just reading and thinking and praying? How often do we give a large chunk of one day each week to God?

As Rabbi Arthur Lavinsky from Beth El Congregation said, "The Sabbath is as much God's gift to us as it is our gift to God."

There are a variety of reasons why I like to go to church, but one of them is, I don't get telephone calls. I leave the cell phone in the car. I do things I normally would never do during the week. I make small talk with people. I sit, listen to a sermon and think about something other than my job or some pressing personal issue. I pray with people about their problems, which often make mine seem like a hangnail in comparison.

I even sing, which often sends the people near me under the pews, covering their ears.

Usually, I have a pretty good time.

"What about our families?" Yahner asked. "Whatever happened to the family meal? How about everyone just sitting down to eat together at least once on Sunday?"

But what about the soccer games and practices? Or golf? Or the bosses who remind us that we need to be ready to close that deal on Monday morning, so we better prepare on Sunday?

"Our world is competitive," said Jim Colledge, pastor of the Hudson Community Chapel. "We think if we don't have our kids practicing on Sunday, some other team is and we'll be at a disadvantage when we play. With traveling teams, even grade-school kids are going all over the place."

We may think if our business isn't always open—well, the other guy is open and we'll lose customers. Many women never get a break, as meals have to be cooked, diapers changed, children watched and beds made every day of the week.

Colledge mentioned research that shows how our productivity drops as much as 50 percent if we work more than six days in a row. It's an even sharper decrease after 10 to 14 consecutive days.

"God built us to rest once a week," he said. "If we can just stop long enough to listen to our bodies, we know that's true."

At one time, there were Blue Laws, requiring most businesses to be closed on Sunday. That slowed things down a bit. Before electricity, most people lived on farms and ceased working when the sun went down because it was dark and they couldn't see.

Now, the days and nights blur together, and it feels like many of us are trapped on a roller-coaster.

"It takes courage to get off," Loar said. "So often, we try to fit God into our schedule, and once a week, we should build our schedule around making time for God. And we'd feel better for it."

Saturday, October 12, 2002

Scapegoat Needed? Use God

God told me to write this story with a special message for you: Send me at least $25.

No, wait a minute, I think I'm hearing another word from On High . . .

That's right, $50.

If you're reading this, God wants you to mail me $50, and you'd better do it right now, because God is about to raise the price.

That's because God wants me to have a Lexus.

Oh, God also told me not to pay taxes, not to pay any bills at a restaurant, not to pay for anything.

Know why?

That's because God wants me to be happy, and he wants you to pay for it.

OK, you probably get the point.

God doesn't need me or anyone else to stick up for him, but I've had it.

I've had it with headlines such as: "God Told Him To Do It," about the guy charged with kidnapping then-14-year-old Elizabeth Smart.

I've had it with another headline that screamed: "REVELATION MAY HAVE LED TO GIRL'S ABDUCTION." I've got a revelation of my own: What a load of manure.

I've had it with some guy saying God told him to kidnap a young girl, to blow up a building, to leave his wife and kids for no good reason.

I've had it with God being reduced to The Great Excuse in the Sky.

When a criminal blames God, I sometimes hear from some people who say: "That proves it. All you religious people are nuts, and the world would be a better place if they shut down every house of worship."

Remember when the Son of Sam was on a murderous rampage in New York? He said he received his orders from a dog.

Should we kill all dogs?

Suppose I drive my car into a restaurant and five people die. I say it's Toyota's fault, because if they hadn't made my Camry, then I never would have done it.

Don't blame me.

Blame the dealership. They never should have sold a basket case like me a car.

Blame what I ate for breakfast. It put me in a bad mood.

Blame my premature baldness. It made me an object of ridicule at a young age, which led me to be angry at society.

Given those circumstances, it's perfectly understandable that I'd drive my car through a restaurant window.

If that doesn't work, I can always drag out the God Made Me Do It defense.

After all, God has yet to show up in court and deny the charge. That makes him an easy target, the perfect scapegoat.

So it figures that the guy charged with kidnapping Elizabeth Smart calls himself "a prophet of God," and God told him to "gather seven young wives."

Deranged people do hear strange voices, but those words sure don't come from God.

Want to know what God says?

Unless you take a verse out of context and twist it for your own purpose, the scriptures of every major faith don't tell anyone to kidnap 14-year-old girls, to shoot people at abortion clinics, to turn yourself into a suicide bomber, to have affairs, to steal, to gossip or to gamble away your savings.

A lot of people have done a lot of destructive things in the name of God over the centuries. But does that really mean that God told them to?

Ever have someone at work tell you, "The boss wants you to stay late and help me do this"?

Then you discover it wasn't the boss, it was the guy trying to manipulate you. He just borrowed the name of the boss for his own agenda.

People have always used God that way, and probably always will. That's why we need to know that God calls people to give more than they receive, to be faithful, to be patient, to be forgiving, to strive for peace and honesty.

There once was a TV preacher who called himself "The Prophet." For $25, he'd send you "the blessing plan." As my friend told me, "You got the plan, and The Prophet made the profit."

It's been like that from the beginning of time. Just don't blame God for it.

Saturday, March 22, 2003

Two Pastors Struggle Across a Racial Gap to Build a Strong, Lasting Bond

The first pastor comes from a broken home, his father divorcing his mother when he was 11.

When he was 17, his 14-year-old sister died.

When he was 22, his mother died of cancer.

He was raised mostly by his grandmother, who took him into the projects, where she ran a Bible study.

The second pastor is the son of a pastor, a middle-class kid who was a high school football star from a two-parent home.

His church is his father's church; his faith came from his parents.

Two pastors.

One white, one black.

Two friends.

The first pastor admits he is "from a dysfunctional background."

Many would guess this would be the black pastor.

Many would be wrong.

The first pastor is Knute Larson of The Chapel. He comes across as white, solid, middle-class. A guy who looks good in a suit, can talk the corporate lingo and understands how business is done from the mall to the boardroom.

But not much in his life prepared him for that.

The second pastor, the one who followed his father into the pulpit, is Ron Fowler of the Arlington Church of God. He has a heart for the city. He knows the dark alleys where drug deals are made, while at the same time he has served on the boards of corporations and the Akron Public Schools.

People see Fowler and Larson together and want to put them in a box. The inner-city black preacher, the middle-class white minister.

Other than their ages—Fowler is 64, Larson is 59—and professions, what would they have in common?

Actually, that should be more than enough, if we ever could set race aside. And that's exactly what these two men have done, demonstrating how Jesus Christ can cut through chains of color.

The friendship didn't happen by accident.

About 15 years ago, the phone rang in Fowler's office. It was Larson, who had met him at a couple of conferences.

A few minutes into the conversation, Larson said, "I'd like to be friends."

Those who have seen Larson only in his TV advertisements or just heard him speak from the pulpit don't realize that he is a very shy man. Small talk doesn't come easily. Expressing his feelings seems to go against every fiber in his body.

As Fowler said, "Once you get to know Knute, he's a genuine, witty guy. But he can come off as aloof at first. He's very guarded."

Growing up in a home where a father leaves . . . where a sister dies . . . where a mother fights and eventually dies from cancer . . . that can cause anyone to draw inward.

Despite the fact that Larson was president of virtually every high school and college class and captain of his athletic teams, his leadership style hardly fit his name. He is no Knute Rockne; there is no rousing Win One for the Gipper Speech, complete with tears, from this guy. Larson is a man who earns respect through his quiet competence, his dedication, the aura of stability that emanates from him.

Fowler noticed Larson from a distance—especially how Larson was able to survive after taking over The Chapel in

1982 from the Rev. David Burnham, a very popular preacher. Burnham's father, Carl, had started The Chapel in 1934.

"When Knute came in, I'd figured he'd last a year, maybe two at the most," Fowler said. "That usually happens after you follow someone like Burnham. They take you to the slaughter."

The first few years were rocky, but Larson endured and then thrived.

But what did this have to do with Fowler, with Arlington Church of God? What was the angle? What could be in it for Larson, for The Chapel?

"Why do you want to do this?" Fowler asked.

"Because I feel guilty," Larson said.

The moment those words left Larson's lips, he wanted to take them back.

"I knew I wasn't explaining myself very well," Larson said.

Said Fowler: "Guilt is never a good reason to do anything. Nothing out of guilt lasts."

Larson knew exactly how he sounded, like a wimpy white liberal trying to make up for slavery.

"What I meant, is that I have failed in this area," he said. "I should try to do this out of the love for Jesus Christ."

At this point, Fowler thought of two things.

The first was a relationship with a prominent white preacher from many years before. He supposedly wanted to be friends, but Fowler felt he was being used. He was the token black. He never forgot that, and he wondered if that was what Larson had in mind.

The second was The Girl at the Creek.

The little white girl.

"She's why I'm still alive," he said.

Fowler's family used to go to Tinkers Creek in Bedford. His mother told him not to go into the water.

"I was eight years old," he said. "I went in the water."

And the current dragged him under.

"Then I felt these arms pulling me up," he said. "It was a white girl. She saved my life. The amazing thing was, the white people would always leave when we came to picnic and swim. This was long before integration."

But not that time.

Fowler remembered someone extending a white hand to him, and he took it, a white hand from a girl he never saw again.

"OK," Fowler told Larson. "We'll get together and talk."

Larson had his own story, one about his grandmother.

Her name was Rosa Engle.

"She loved the Lord," Larson said, "and would teach a Bible class every week in the projects of Harrisburg (Pa.)."

And young Larson went along. This was the only time he was around black people, and his grandmother was doing this back in the 1950s, long before it was politically correct.

Larson also thought of an incident that took place at the church in Ashland where he was pastor before coming to The Chapel.

"We had this elderly, white-haired deacon," Larson said. "One day, this African-American family came to church, one of the few in town. Afterwards, I talked to them for a while. When they left, the deacon told me, 'I really respect you because you treated them like a regular family.' The guy had no idea what he was saying, how insulting that was."

Somehow, we have to get past all that, Larson thought.

"Most people have the wrong idea of how to build friendships between the races," Fowler said. "They think you start a project, then get blacks and whites involved, and they'll become friends. But what usually happens is the friendships last only as long as the project. Then everyone moves on."

Which is why Fowler and Larson agreed to meet at least once a month to do nothing more than get to know each other.

After a while, Larson believed they had hit a wall. Some strained small talk. Some shop talk. Some decent lunches.

But no real relationship.

"You don't trust me," Larson said.

Fowler told him about the broken promises from the white church leader. Larson talked about his lack of exposure to blacks, about how he desperately wanted to bridge the gap, but had no idea how to do it.

Fowler told Larson how he had no intention of being "black window dressing."

That meeting was the breakthrough because they spoke to each other like men. Men who didn't hide behind the fact that they came from different races. Men who decided to stare those differences in the eye and not blink until they had talked them through.

There were questions such as, "Why do blacks like that?" Naive questions from Larson, but honest questions.

Fowler appreciated Larson dropping his guard and being willing to sound stupid so he could try to learn. Fowler gave Larson a history lesson on slavery, which led to a discussion of different worship styles.

"The black church was the only place of joy during the days of slavery," Fowler said. "It's why our music is so joyful, while the preaching is so interactive with the congregations—just as so many white worship services go back to the European tradition of quiet reverence for God."

The key to their relationship was that both pastors were from successful churches.

"The idea wasn't the big white church adopts the poor minority church," Larson said. "It was two men getting to know each other, and then maybe us being able to model a friendship for the people in our churches."

The Chapel has about 8,000 members and is embarking on a

$25 million expansion with a second church in Green.

The Arlington Church of God has about 1,000 members and is building a $1.8 million addition to its Christian school.

Neither church "needs" the other, although Fowler said he had to fight some suspicion on the part of a few other black pastors who wondered if his friendship with Larson was really a ploy to get financial support from The Chapel.

As time has passed, so have those whispers.

"Only equals can be true friends," Fowler said.

Fowler and Larson both found that they had far more in common than they had differences based on race.

Larson talked about how he has a real heart for people who are grieving, how he hates those who come up to someone who has just lost a loved one and offer a trite saying or a Bible verse.

He recalled a woman telling his mother, "I know that it's hard for you to lose your daughter, but you never know. Maybe God did this because she could have grown up to be a prostitute."

How's that for words of comfort?

"In the church of my youth, we'd sing, 'Every day with Jesus is sweeter than the day before,'" Larson said. "But that's just not true. For some things, there are no easy answers."

Larson talked about how he hates legalism, how we should obey God much like we do our spouses—doing things out of love, "not out of fear of being yelled at."

Fowler talked about an Akron before the civil rights laws, an Akron where he had to watch movies from the balcony, because only the "regular white people" were allowed down below.

"What astounded me was how Ron could talk about those things with passion, but not bitterness," Larson said. "He wants to solve problems. I just wish he had more of a chance to mediate disputes, something like Jesse Jackson does. He has such wisdom, such an understanding of people."

Fowler and Larson have been friends for 12 years, meeting

face to face at least once a month and speaking on the phone a few times each week.

Their churches have joint services a few times each year, and also have a shared Bible class, a retreat and other activities.

"The classes and other activities is where the real friendships have evolved," Fowler said. "The people at our church really like Knute and some of the people they've met from The Chapel."

Larson says much the same about Fowler and his congregation.

Yet The Chapel remains overwhelmingly white; Arlington is nearly all black.

"A lot of it is just cultural," Fowler said. "Certain people are just used to certain kinds of worship. What Knute and I try to do is explain to our people that there are different kinds of worship."

Such as?

"When some people come to our church for the first time and hear all the gospel music and the clapping, they almost treat it like a show," Fowler said. "They like the entertainment, but they miss the worship, and that makes me angry."

And when some people attend The Chapel for the first time?

"They (Chapel members) are more subdued than we are," Fowler said. "People will tell me, 'That's OK, but that's not church.' I'll say, 'You are absolutely wrong. That was church, just a different style of church.' But it's still church because Knute and I preach the Bible."

Larson says he would like to attract more minorities to his church. Fowler wishes he had more whites in his pews.

On certain days, when the two churches come together, it happens.

"And it's beautiful," Fowler said. "It's a hope for the future."

Larson and Fowler now speak together at schools and churches in the cause of racial reconciliation.

Race is only one of their contrasts. Larson stands ramrod-straight and is rail-thin, looking much taller than his 5-foot-11 frame. That's especially true when he stands next to the 5-foot-7, roly-poly Fowler.

Fowler smiles easily and hugs everyone, even those he has just met.

Larson sometimes struggles when dealing with strangers.

"Of course we're different," said Larson. "We used to think that if we just brought whites and blacks together, all the racial problems would vanish. . . . There were a lot of shattered expectations from the civil rights era. Only now are we seeing how deep are the problems and beginning to pick up the pieces again."

Fowler thought about how his relationship with Larson developed.

"Hey, we all say dumb things," he said. "We all do dumb things. We all have certain racist attitudes. But if we put Jesus Christ at the center of our hearts, we can overcome that. I believe that's what Knute and I have done."

Sunday, September 10, 2000

FAITH

Girl's Encounter With Angels Rings True

The girl saw angels.

Six angels, dressed in long white robes.

Female angels stroking the foreheads of six dead teen-agers.

That's what Katie Gonzalez talked about upon her release from Children's Hospital Medical Center of Akron. Katie was the lone survivor of a December 27 car wreck in rural Wayne County, near Creston.

Seven people in a 1996 Buick Park Avenue Electra; six dead.

"That vision was a very vivid experience for her," said Donald Kuntz, the pastor of Creston United Methodist Church.

Kuntz spoke with Katie in the hospital, and he is convinced the girl is sincere. He said the 14-year-old girl first told the story of her vision to her sister Leslie.

"It was right after Katie heard that all her friends in the car were dead," he said.

So what do we make of this?

A teen-age girl endures an incredible life-and-death experience. Everyone dies; she lives. Maybe her brain created the image of these angels, sort of as a defense mechanism. Teen-age girls are prone to flights of fancy, so why not angels?

Certainly, it's easier to believe that a mind plays tricks than it is to actually think that what Katie saw was, well, angels.

"Part of having faith in God is faith in things we can't see," said the Rev. Norm Douglas, co-founder of the nonprofit Heart to Heart Communications.

That's true.

"Some people are really into angels, like they find them under every bush, and you have to be suspicious about that," said Douglas. "But reading this story, it seemed different. I can't prove what she said is right, but I can't disprove it, either. To me, her story sounded very real."

In the Bible, there are at least 42 references to angels. They also are in the Torah, the Book of Mormon and other religious literature.

Few people of faith doubt their existence, yet how many of us really expect to see one? Or even talk to someone who had an encounter with an angel, even though the book of Hebrews says some of us have entertained angels without realizing it?

Dr. Diana Swoope is the assistant pastor of the Arlington Church of God. She heard Katie Gonzalez's story and thought of something that happened to her when she was only 6 years old.

"I saw an angel," Swoope said.

Really?

"He was huge, definitely a man," she said. "He was in front of our house, like he was guarding it. He had on a white robe. I only saw him once, but I know I saw him."

And?

"I know there are ministering angels, messenger angels and guardian angels," she said. "There are angels that usher us to heaven, so I tend to believe what the girl said."

Katie Gonzalez said: "Before this, I smoked and I wasn't very religious."

So it doesn't seem that she had been thinking about angels

prior to the accident. She just knows what she saw: six female angels caring for her six dead friends.

"I believe that whatever drives that girl to Jesus Christ is good," said the Rev. Randy Baker of Akron Bible Church. "I never saw Jesus, but I believe in him. I keep my mind open. When I've made mission trips to India, you hear more stories like this than we do here."

To most of us, there is the real world, and . . .

The real world.

But most religions insist there is a spirit world, only we're too busy and too caught up in ourselves to notice.

"People in hospices tend to talk more about seeing Jesus, or feeling the presence of God or one of His angels," Kuntz said. "At the end of our lives, or when we are close to death of a loved one, I think we become more sensitive to things."

Katie Gonzalez was in the hospital for 17 days. She broke bones in both legs, suffered a partially collapsed lung and a bruised spleen. At one point, doctors thought they'd have to amputate a foot. The foot was saved, but it's still not certain whether she ever will be able to walk without some type of aid.

"Those angels were God's way of telling her that He was there for her and her friends," Kuntz said. "Those ladies in white were a great comfort to her. To someone in Katie's situation, that's very important."

Whether we believe it, or not.

Saturday, February 3, 2001

Are you lonely?

Most of us would say no.

Unless we were being honest.

Then we would say . . . maybe.

Or . . . sometimes.

How many of us can call someone and say, "Hey, I'm kind of lonely, I just thought I'd check in with you."

Thought so.

There are times when I've called people, when I just wanted to hear a friendly voice. There were times when I knew that I was getting sick of just being with me, and I wanted someone to talk with me, maybe pray with me.

And I wimped out.

I made small talk.

Someone asked, "How you doing?"

I said, "Fine. Everything's fine."

They said, "You sure?"

I said, "I'm fine, why? Don't I sound fine?"

They said, "Hey, I was just asking."

Ever have a conversation like that?

Bet most of us have been there. Bet most of us hate to admit it. Bet most of us wish we could tell someone, "I sort of feel alone."

Just like that, be honest about it.

Sounds easy, but it makes us feel weak. We should be able to handle ourselves and our moods, right?

People of faith can fall into the trap of thinking they're not supposed to be lonely.

After all, we have God.

And didn't God say, "I will never leave you or forsake you?"

It's right there, in the Old Testament Book of Joshua, first chapter.

So what's the problem?

Some people read Scriptures and start beating themselves up.

"I must be selfish," they think.

"My faith must be failing," they think.

They think too much.

They forget about Jesus crying from the cross, "My God, my God, why have you forsaken me?"

It's right there in the Book of Mark: chapter 15, verse 34.

I always thought Jesus picked a dozen disciples to do more than just train them to start a new church. He wanted some buddies. He needed company. He had to know they'd drive him crazy at times, but it would still be worth it.

Better than just being alone.

Jesus used to hang out at the home of two sisters named Martha and Mary. Martha liked to cook and be the hostess. Mary liked to talk to Jesus, to listen to him, to treat him as a special guest.

Jesus liked them both, so much so that he insisted Martha stop worrying about dinner and come do what Mary was doing.

He had male friends and female friends.

Christians believe Jesus is the son of God, yet the Bible makes it clear that he needed friends, too. Friends who didn't just want things from him. Friends who seemed to accept him, who didn't demand he do the loaves and fishes miracle again, or that he heal everyone in the neighborhood.

Jesus sought out friends with whom he could just chill out, not do much of anything with other than just be himself.

I sense we've lost that.

We know a lot of people . . .

And a lot of people know us . . .

But how many of us really know much about each other?

There are work friends. Church friends. Family friends. Sports friends. Hobby friends.

But real friends?

Not as many as we think.

Part of the problem is we don't make time for friends, and they often don't have time for us. People with kids often feel like little more than a taxi service. People with older relatives sometimes think they are an EMS squad, always on call, always waiting for the next crisis to hit.

Why do some of us look back at friends from school, from the drama club, the band or the sports teams with a real sense of closeness?

Because we spent a lot of time with no cell phones ringing, no buzzers beeping, no appointments to keep, no deadlines to make.

We were with those friends in cafeterias, buses, fast food joints and the mall. We talked about real issues and silly stuff.

And those of us who didn't have friends like that in school may still ache from that lack of connection.

I sense if we worked just half as hard at friendships as we do at our jobs, we'd have more friends, better marriages, closer families. But it starts with making time to be with the people we care about—for no other reason than we care about them.

In the Book of Genesis, it was God who said, "It's not good for man to be alone."

Guess he should know.

Saturday, May 17, 2003

Annie Godby Steps Up to the Plate— in Baseball and in Life

How tall is Annie Godby?

"I'm 4-foot-5," she insists.

Maybe she is, or maybe she was measured standing on her toes. It doesn't matter.

Annie Godby is 21 years old, a 12-year veteran of a program called Challenger Baseball. Her favorite player is Nolan Ryan, "because he played so long," she told her mother.

Annie Godby might be the Nolan Ryan of Barberton's Challenger Baseball, the oldest player in the league. She runs out every ground ball despite knees that ache from inflammation of the joints.

In the field, she stands attentively, glove out and ready—even if sometimes she's stationed herself in foul territory.

She doesn't miss a chance to cheer for a teammate, although her voice is usually flat.

"Cool," she likes to say. "Real cool."

Annie Godby is very cool—just ask those who know her.

"She loves to help as much as play," said her coach, Adam Evans. "If a kid is having trouble putting on a batting helmet, Annie is there. She is naturally unselfish."

It's more than that.

Dr. Mark Matthews says Annie is like most people with Down Syndrome. "They are absolutely pure of heart."

Or as her mother said, "We've been together for 21 years, and I've never caught Annie in a lie. Not once."

Pam Godby asked her daughter about that.

"Why lie?" wondered Annie, as if her mother had suggested she should eat mud.

Why lie? Why complain? Why even ask why?

What good does any of it do?

Annie Godby isn't perfect, but there is something indeed pure about her.

It begins with baseball.

Very few of the 500 kids in town this weekend for the Ohio State Challenger Baseball Tournament in Barberton have been playing as long as Annie Godby.

"Baseball is her life," says her mother. "About every day, we go play catch and practice at (Barberton's) Edgewood Park."

Annie Godby has a baseball cap collection. Her current favorite is the red Angels hat. She proudly shows off a picture of herself menacingly holding a bat. It's the MVP trophy for her team.

In Challenger Baseball, every kid reaches first base. Every kid bats every inning. Every kid is made to feel like an MVP, no matter if they are like Annie, in a wheelchair or suffering from some other disorder.

Matthews is one of the leaders of the Barberton program, and as he says, "We make every kid count."

Kids like Annie Godby, kids who are becoming adults in front of our eyes, these young people need to hear that message every day: They count.

Challenger Baseball helps them remember that.

"Next year, I'm too old to play," says Annie Godby. "But I get to help and coach."

Like so many veteran big-leaguers who sense their careers ending, Annie Godby just wants to stay around the game. With Challenger, she can do that as long as she likes.

Annie Godby has a baseball card collection neatly arranged by team. She has every Backstreet Boys CD. She likes to sing

"Achy Breaky Heart," by Billy Ray Cyrus. She loves to read a series of books called *The Baby Sitters Club*. Her favorite movie is *The Lion King*.

She is 21.

She has one foot in childhood, another in adulthood.

She is bright enough to tell her Bible study class at Barberton's Johnson Church, "Jesus is like a compass. A compass always points north. It tells you which way to go."

But she has Down Syndrome, a chromosome abnormality that often shows itself in mental retardation and other defects. That means she is usually challenged in some areas. People with this condition tend to speak in a monotone. They have dry throats, which can make them difficult to understand until you spend time with them.

It also causes joint pain, breathing problems and sometimes the early development of Alzheimer's. She was hospitalized for nearly two weeks this spring with a mood disorder in which she was disoriented, depressed and just not the usually resilient Annie Godby.

As much as the medical care, the coming of the baseball season seemed to snap her out of it.

Hand her a piece of paper and ask her to write what the game means to her, and she thinks for several moments and then prints: "The goal of baseball is playing with my friends. Next is be a good sportsman and finally inspire or inspiration."

Ain't that the truth?

Annie Godby knows she has Down Syndrome. She knows she will usually be the smallest adult in the room. She knows some people will think she's still a kid, because she looks about 11. She knows life can be very hard.

"She once asked why she was like this," said her mother.

Pam Godby adopted her exactly because she wasn't like every other kid. Pam was a single woman who had worked with handicapped children and asked if she could be a mother to one.

"It took a while, but I became one of the first single mothers granted an adoption in Summit County," she said. "Annie was 4½ months. I didn't ask specifically for a Down Syndrome child, but I was interested in taking care of someone with special needs."

Pam took Annie to see a movie called *Simon Birch*, about a dwarf who is the hero. They have rented it and watched it several more times. It means a lot to Annie, to see someone who is small become popular, someone whose size was supposed to be a disadvantage, yet it became an asset.

"Usually, I like how tall I am," said Annie Godby.

"Some people believe that Down Syndrome kids can't have much more than a 50 IQ, that they plateau," said Pam Godby. "But I don't see that with Annie. She keeps learning new things. I refuse to let anyone put a limit on her."

She just graduated from Norton High's special needs program. Her next stop is Weaver School, where she'll take part in job and skill training.

Pam Godby has worked in day care for years, but she's between jobs now, partly because of all the time consumed by taking care of Annie's recent medical problems.

Life also has been a struggle for Pam, who lost a leg to cancer 17 years ago. There are financial pressures, health issues, feelings of loneliness.

When Annie Godby notices her mother feeling low, she often says, "I love you, Mom."

"Why?" asks Pam.

"Because you're my mom," says Annie.

Why bother to say anything else?

Wednesday, August 6, 2003

Do Pets Get Into Heaven?

Will there be animals in heaven?

"Tell me this, will there be allergies in the afterlife?" asked Rabbi Arthur Lavinsky of Beth El Congregation in Akron.

There are many allergic people who hope not. Many of them would love to cuddle up with the animals in heaven that they couldn't hug on Earth.

Joni Eareckson Tada is a popular evangelist who uses a wheelchair. She recently packed The Chapel in Akron, where she talked about her faith in the face of incredible physical disabilities.

She also wrote a book called *Heaven . . . Your Real Home*, in which she wrote: "Animals in heaven? Yes. I think animals are some of God's best ideas . . . I'm not talking about my pet schnauzer, Scrappy, dying and going to heaven . . . I'm talking about new animals fit for a new order of things."

Tada was deluged with angry mail from people wanting to know why their pets wouldn't be in heaven. She has since revised her words, saying if God wants your pet in heaven, your pet will be in heaven.

But is that true?

"I have no idea," said Terry Holley, pastor of Medina's Heartland Church. "If they are there, it's not for the same reason that we are. I know when a little kid loses her dog, she likes to think her pet will be in heaven."

Many adults have the same dreams.

"There is scripture about the wolf laying down with the lamb [Isaiah 11: 6-9]," said Jerry Durham from Wooster's Church of the Savior. "But animals don't have souls, so I don't know what to say."

That seems to be the opinion of most clergy.

"Animals don't have souls," said The Chapel's Knute Larson. "But if God wants animals to be there, then He'll have animals in heaven and it could be fun."

Psalm 50:11 says, "I know every bird in the mountains, and the creatures of the field are mine."

This much is certain: Like us, animals belong to God.

"The difference is that we're made in the likeness of God. Animals are not," said Bill Cunningham of Medina's First Baptist Church. "So I'd say there would be no animals in heaven. Christ came to redeem mankind, not angels or animals."

Dr. Jay Groat from the First Congregational Church in Akron has another opinion.

"Every Father's Day, I give myself a break from doing a sermon and just take questions from the people," he said. "Someone usually asks about animals in heaven. More people wonder about that than most clergy think."

And the answer is . . .

"Of course," Groat said. "When I was young, I had a Norwegian elkhound named Eric. I had some pretty lonely times when it seemed that Eric was my only friend. I really believe I'll see Eric again. I know there's no Biblical basis for this, but being with Eric would be a piece of salvation for me, and I think God takes that into consideration."

God is rather mum on this subject.

The Bible says God made man to rule over the animals. It also says He knows every sparrow that falls.

In the book of Jonah, God says He not only spared 120,000 "who don't know their right from their left (because they're children)," but also "many cattle as well." (No other animals are mentioned in that reference.)

"Some of the Biblical verses about animals is a vision of a perfect age," Lavinsky said. "I just think a place where people all get along would be the greatest accomplishment."

In his book, *Resurrection*, Hank Hanegraaff (the radio Bible Answerman) writes, "The Garden of Eden was populated by animals, thus there is a precedent for believing that Eden restored will be populated by animals . . . Some of the keenest thinkers from C.S. Lewis to Peter Kreeft are convinced pets will be restored in the resurrection."

Father Gordon Yahner of St. Hilary Catholic Church in Fairlawn was stumped at first by the question. Then he said: "All I know for sure about heaven is our union with God will be way beyond our greatest expectations, and if that includes animals, so be it."

Saturday, May 26, 2001

Don't Let Life Scare You

My scariest day since Sept. 11 was about two weeks ago.

I was driving home from covering a Browns game, and there was a drunk in an SUV, weaving across three lanes of Interstate 77. I held my breath for about 10 minutes before the guy finally pulled off the ramp at Pleasant Valley Road.

Have you ever been in that situation?

You see someone leaning forward over the steering wheel, his nose nearly into the windshield, trying to see and keep the car on the road.

He knows he's drunk.

You know he's drunk.

And neither of you knows where he's going.

If you want to be afraid of something, that's it. Driving—still the most dangerous activity for most of us.

This is not to diminish the fear that must feel like a fist around the heart to those in New York. I don't still smell the smoke. I don't know anyone who died in the World Trade Center. I don't live in a city where part of it was just reduced to rubble.

Yet, even in New York, most people refuse to be paralyzed. My friends in that town tell me they have buried what remained of the dead, dusted off their lives, and moved on—putting one foot in front of the other.

It's what we have to do.

Especially if you claim to be a person of faith, if you really believe there is a God and He's in charge.

But some of the most fearful, angst-ridden people say they believe in God. They try to figure out God's hand in all this, then crawl deeper in their mental bunkers. They think that the world is going to hell, or Jesus is coming again—or maybe both.

They stare at the word "anthrax" in the headlines and are terrified of opening the mail. Or going to the post office. Or touching a stamp.

They don't want to fly, because who knows what those thugs may do next?

They see evil and danger lurking everywhere.

They say God's teachings are important, yet they act as if they've never read the Bible or the Quran.

Scripture is packed with stories of destruction and redemption, of grace in the face of violence, betrayal and tragedy. And of men and women of God enduring it, and sometimes using it to bring glory to the creator of the universe.

From Moses to the apostles, Scripture teaches that part of following God is doing things that are out of our comfort zone, of sometimes being downright scared.

Bible scholars say the words "Fear not" or "Don't be afraid" appear more than 300 times.

Because God knows, we do fear.

And God knows, that often leads to panic, and then some form of spiritual surrender.

Some people stare at CNN all day. They've seen a thousand replays of those jets crashing into the World Trade Center.

Why?

Or they read every word about anthrax.

Why?

You want to know what is most likely to kill you? Not a bomb. Not anthrax. Not even a gun.

A heart attack. Cancer. Depression, which doctors now insist leads to physical problems. Those are the real dangers.

That's assuming you're not in a car wreck on the way to the hospital.

Those who want to spread their faith are supposed to live vibrant, hopeful lives. They are supposed to not carelessly put themselves at risk, but also refuse to cower in the corner the moment there is a strange noise in the house.

In some respects, Osama bin Laden is right. This is a religious war, but the real battle is raging in our own hearts.

Saturday, October 27, 2001

Even 9/11 Wasn't Enough for Lasting Spirituality

I don't see it.

I don't think the September 11 attacks changed most people, at least those people who live outside New York and Washington.

I don't believe the *Newsweek* story that insists: "We are different now."

Are we? Really? Down deep?

The attack on the World Trade Center and the Pentagon was supposed to shake our world, to cause us to look inside at our hearts and up to God.

For a while, that happened.

But a year later?

Certainly in New York, people are still wounded souls, still spiritually searching, still wanting comfort and a reason to hope.

But how about us?

I hate to admit it, but any growth in my own faith in the past year has been incidental to the attack. I don't plan to spend much time watching all the TV specials, reading the "One Year Later" stories. I will pray for the families of the dead, and for those trying to help the grieving. But I can't even remember the last time I did that.

I'm not alone.

A September 2 survey by the respected Barna Research Group revealed that only 6 percent of Americans said their religious leaders did a "below-average job" responding to the attacks.

But only 12 percent of Americans believe the bombings had "any impact on their faith." Among men, it was a mere 7 percent.

And 67 percent don't plan to do anything special on September 11 to commemorate the dead.

So it appears most people believe pastors, rabbis and imams made a valiant effort to reach out during the crisis, but for some reason, it just didn't take.

Business as usual.

I'm convinced people are hungry for a relationship with God. The bombings may have increased that yearning, but most people didn't seem to find the answers they sought when they came back to their places of worship.

Remember the packed churches, temples and mosques of a year ago? Remember the interfaith prayer services? Remember how God was in vogue for a few weeks, and no one dared try to kick his name out of the Pledge of Allegiance or anywhere else?

Now what do you see?

Business as usual.

Calls to several local churches revealed that attendance is about the same, or perhaps up slightly, from last September 11. There has been no huge increase.

The exception seems to be at Temple Israel. Rabbi David Lipper said attendance for this month's Holy Days services is expected to be much greater than in the recent past. And the terrorist attacks, here and in Israel, have something to do with that.

Next week, there will be many special services marking the anniversary of the attacks, but I wonder if they will mean very much to most of us.

Why didn't people stay in church after they came back a year ago?

One theory is that they found the same church they once had

left. The sermons were boring and not relevant to real life. Or the people were petty, and church seemed more like a social club where everyone seemed to know the magic handshake and the secret password, except for you.

So often, phony church people and cardboard services get between us and a real God, and I'm sure that happened in some cases. I also know that some people spend far more time shopping for a new car or a new dress than they do a good church.

Pastor Jim Colledge of Hudson Community Chapel mentioned the old saying that some Americans can endure almost anything—just as long as it doesn't last more than a few weeks.

The Rev. Paul Schindler of St. Bernard Catholic Church in Akron said it shouldn't take a bombing to bring people back to the Lord. If it's just the crisis that drew them to church, then people will leave as soon as it appears things have calmed down.

Which was exactly what happened. The Barna survey revealed that everything from church attendance to Bible reading to prayer stayed almost the same from right before the attacks to a year later.

People came back to church, but they didn't stay.

Pastor Knute Larson of The Chapel in Akron said that once the initial sermons about heaven and why there is evil in the world were delivered, then came the talk about dealing with and repenting for sins—topics some people just don't want to hear about.

Faith is a process, and at times it can be painful.

That's another unpopular lesson.

Pastor Joey Johnson of Akron's House of the Lord said the terrorist attacks had "absolutely no spiritual impact" at his church. "America is such a drowsy nation." he said. "That just wasn't enough of a wake-up call because most people were not personally touched by it."

So it was easy to ignore the attacks after awhile.

George Barna authored the survey cited here, and he said his findings say "something about the spiritual complacency of the American public."

That's evident, and so is the inability of religious institutions to reach people with their message.

Saturday, September 7, 2002

God's Message to Job: You Can't Have it All

Many of us grew up hearing about the patience of Job.

At least in my mind, he was the long-suffering, never-complaining guy who could handle everything hell threw his way.

Just the thought of Job made me feel like a wimp.

Then I read his story in the Bible and discovered that most of us have more in common with Job than we think.

Ever been in a lousy situation that wasn't your fault? Maybe you or someone in your family became gravely ill. Maybe a business failed and a job was lost, and you really had nothing to do with it.

You truly were in the wrong place at the wrong time.

Then some "friends" came along, supposedly to console, but all they did was lay down the blame: "You must have done *something* to cause it. We all reap what we sow, right? Isn't that in the Bible somewhere?"

That's what happened to Job.

In fact, most of the Book of Job is about his discussion with three rather miserable characters who make you say, "If these are friends, I'd rather have kidney stones."

The Bible says Job was a terrific guy, God's favorite. In fact, God brags about Job in the heavens. Satan hears this, and says Job is faithful because God keeps blessing him.

"Let me put the guy through the wringer," Satan says, "and then he will spit in your face."

OK, that's not a direct biblical quote, but you get the idea. It's as if Satan is trash-talking to God, and Job ends up in the middle of some strange, supernatural test. I try not to think about this, because I just don't get it, and it can be pretty scary.

Anyway, God lets it happen. Satan takes away Job's farm, his cattle, his wealth, his children. Finally, Job is covered with boils and has other dreadful diseases.

If that's not enough, his wife offers this advice, "Why don't you curse God and die!"

Job had to be thinking, "Hey, honey, you have a nice day, too."

How many of us have been there? Maybe no one actually spoke out as Job's wife did, but we know they thought it. They wrote us off. They believed we just couldn't supply what was expected of us.

Then came well-meaning people with stupid advice.

A dim bulb named Bildad says Job's problems were the result of his sins, or his children's sins, "and God gave you the penalty of their sins."

Thanks for sharing.

Job hears this and says, "My body is clothed with worms and scabs, my skin is broken and festering . . . my eyes will never see happiness again."

It would seem a little tenderness is in order, but a wretched soul named Eliphaz says, "Blessed is the man whom God corrects, so do not despise the discipline of the Almighty."

Job doesn't disagree with that statement—he just wonders what he has done to deserve this. He calls out to God, but hears nothing.

At one point, Job says: "How can I argue with Him?"

Because God doesn't answer.

Another time, Job moans, "I loathe my very life . . . and speak in the bitterness of my soul . . . what charges do You have against me?"

But there is nothing from God.

Just more misery.

Ever been there?

Job calls himself "a laughingstock to my friends."

He tells one of his friends, "You smear me with lies; you are worthless physicians, all of you."

He becomes so depressed that he says, "I wish I'd died before any eyes ever saw me."

What I love about Job is that he acts like most of us would in his situation. He questions himself. He questions God. Most of the time, he receives no answers, just silence. He has doubts.

And other people just don't get it.

Job cries to the Lord, "I've been wronged, but I get no response. I cry for help, there is no justice."

In the past few weeks, I've had a close friend diagnosed with a serious form of cancer. Another friend lost his wife, the mother of his young children. A third friend recently buried a child.

None of these people did anything "wrong." Misery just happened, period.

Like Job, we can ask *why*, but don't count on a reply.

The Book of Job ends with God appearing.

Rather than answer Job, the Almighty asks Job questions such as: "Where were you when I laid the Earth's foundation? Have you ever given orders to the morning? Or shown the dawn its place? Does the rain have a father? From whose womb comes ice?"

God then spends a lot of time talking about animals, saying things such as, "Do you know when the mountain goat gives birth?"

God doesn't address any of Job's concerns.

God basically says, "I'm God; you're not."

Job is awe-struck. "I'm unworthy," he says. "How can I reply to you? I put my hand over my mouth."

Some people try to put a phony smile on Job's face, as God gives him an even bigger farm, more cattle and a better family at the end of the book.

But that's really not the story.

Rather, it's about suffering and the dumb things we say to people who are in the midst of it. And it's about how God's ways are not our ways, and the sooner we come to grips with that, the better.

Like Job, we may even know all that, but trying to live that way isn't easy.

Saturday, January 12, 2002

DECISIONS

Accurate, But Not True:
Omitting Key Facts is Lying

Ever find a piece of your past that makes you wince?

I did.

Making it worse, I had completely forgotten about it, because it's proof I lied.

Actually, it is a newspaper story from 1986, someone's review of a play I had written. It was a well-written review, more than fair, and I should have been pleased with it.

The headline read: "Staged reading shows polish, flaws."

I didn't find the original review. Rather, while looking for something else, I discovered a photocopy, where the headline proclaimed: "Staged reading shows polish."

As I stared at that, I remembered the original headline, and I remembered I had conveniently cut out the word "flaws" before making copies to send theaters with the revised script, hoping to persuade someone to do a major production.

As I stared at the photocopy, my stomach began to feel queasy.

That's because I remembered something else I did: I cut out a few paragraphs that said some negative things about the play.

I lied.

I suppose I can justify it by saying, "Hey, everything on the paper is true, the 90 percent of it still there. I didn't alter any sentences."

I knew better then, and I know better now.

I had a friend named Ron Grinker, who passed away several years ago. He was a devout Jew, a respected National Basketball Association agent. His favorite line was, "It's accurate, but not true."

He meant that the information was correct, but other key parts of the story had been left out.

Accurate, but not true.

I plead guilty.

For what it's worth, nothing else happened to the play, despite my schemes to get it noticed. A savvy director didn't need a review to see there were flaws; the script revealed plenty of them.

I hadn't looked at the play for at least 10 years. But as I paged through it a few weeks ago, I realize much of it was a rip-off. Not in content, but in tone. I was doing a very bad imitation of David Mamet, who wrote *American Buffalo* and *Glengarry Glen Ross*.

The play has an embarrassing number of obscenities, and as I look back on it, I'm glad it's forgotten and hope it stays that way.

But a bigger issue was the lust I had to push my career forward, and the corners I was willing to cut to make it happen.

Two years ago, a football coach was hired at Notre Dame, then was fired when it was discovered he had lied on his resume, claiming to have played college football when he did not. There also were questions about some of the other background he provided.

The coach said he had "forgotten" to update his resume. By this stage of his career, he had established himself, and it didn't matter if he had played college football.

Like many journalists, I took him to the woodshed in print,

completely forgetting how I had wandered into that ethical woodshed several years ago.

It's always easier to hold someone else to a higher standard.

Part of Psalm 12 reads: "Everyone lies to his neighbor, their flattering lips speak with deception. May the Lord cut off all flattering lips and every boastful tongue." Ouch.

Proverbs 12:22 insists: "The Lord detests lying lips . . ."

Or a pair of scissors doing some deceitful surgery.

I'd like to think I wouldn't do this today, that my spiritual awakening of several years ago has changed me. Then again, I'd like to think I don't gossip, but I know I still listen to it, and I still do it.

And I'm not proud of it.

The good news is forgiveness.

As part of Psalm 5 reads: "You [God] will destroy those who tell lies . . . but by your great mercy, I will come into your house, in reverence I bow down."

Now that is accurate and true.

Saturday, July 26, 2003

The Truth About Absolutes

Do you think there's such a thing as truth?

A lot of us are wondering about that.

Barna Research polled 1,010 people in January 2000 and asked if they agreed with this statement: "There are moral truths that are absolute, meaning these moral truths or principles do not change according to the circumstances."

In that poll, 38 percent believed there is such a thing as moral truth. You can read about this at www.barna.org.

Then came the September 11 attacks, and Barna wondered if that had changed. Did a stark confrontation with what many would say was pure evil—flying passenger jets into crowded buildings—make people think again about right and wrong?

Indeed it did.

"I'd guess more would agree that there is a real truth after September 11," said Jeff Miller, pastor of Chapel Hill Church.

I talked to four other clergy members, and they all backed Miller's opinion. Barna also believed its polling would reveal more people believing in a moral truth.

They were wrong.

Barna was stunned when its own research showed only 22 percent now held a belief in absolutes, according to his poll of November 2001. That was a 16 percent drop.

"I don't know what to make of that, other than maybe some people feel despair after the bombings," said Mark Ruppert, pastor of First Presbyterian Church of Akron.

Maybe we are tempted to believe if the World Trade Center towers can topple, anything can happen.

And if anything can happen, then anything goes.

And if anything goes, then nothing is certain.

"And that saddens me," said Miller, the Chapel Hill pastor.

"This isn't new," said the Rev. Joseph Kraker of St. Vincent's Catholic Church. "I remember hearing lectures in the 1960s about situational ethics. They play mind and word games, where they say, 'What if a women in a Nazi concentration camp has sex with a guard to save the life of her child? Did she do something wrong?'"

Of course, you also can ask, "Is it ever right to sexually abuse a child?"

Kraker and many others in the ministry teach that there is a God who sets standards. There is sin. There is right and wrong.

"God is good and he expects us to do the right things," he said.

The polling revealed that among those under the age of 36, only 13 percent believe in absolute truth.

The highest age group was 37-55, at 28 percent. Hard to believe, but those over 55 were only at 24 percent.

"That just tells me that the secular world is getting out its message and having an even bigger impact than we (ministers) believe," said Ron Fowler, pastor of Arlington Church of God. "Sometimes, it just makes me wonder if we're talking to ourselves."

Fowler and others saw how the attack drove people to church and to their knees. "I really thought there was a search for stability, for core values," he said.

Maybe there was. Maybe people didn't find it. Maybe people just don't know what to think anymore.

"Or maybe we're just too busy to think things through," Miller said. "We live in a society that is just too relativistic."

So often people say, "That may be true for you, but not for me."

Or they say, "You can't tell me what to think."

Or they say, "You're judgmental," and they bring up the biblical passage where Jesus says, "Do not judge, or you too will be judged."

That's from the book of Matthew, although many who use those words have never read the entire passage, which deals with how it's easy to criticize others without looking at ourselves.

"Jesus certainly spoke in absolutes, and that made some people uncomfortable and they walked away," said the Rev. Paul Rosing of Annunciation Catholic Church in Akron.

We may have some moral standards and believe in them to the bottom of our hearts, but we're afraid to say so, fearing what people will think. We live in a world where tolerance is often the gospel preached the most.

When I wrote a column on the sports page about the bottle-throwing at the Browns game, saying it was wrong and dangerous, the response I received was split, about 50-50.

Those making the case of bottle-throwing said, "If the officials hadn't messed up . . ."

As if that made it OK.

You can say you understand why a person did something, but that still doesn't make it moral. Or are there no absolutes, assuming the explanation tugs hard enough at the emotional heart strings?

When Jesus was hauled in front of Pilate, the Roman governor, the subject of truth hung over the room.

The book of John reports Jesus telling Pilate, "For this reason, I was born and for this I came into the world, to testify to the truth. Everyone on the side of the truth listens to me."

Pilate then proved he was a very modern man when he scoffed, "What is truth?"

And a lot of us have been asking that question ever since.

Saturday, January 26, 2002

God Is Not a Hall Pass to Stupidity

Did you hear about the guy who claims that only he can discipline his wife, and he mentions some obscure Old Testament verses as the reason?

The police, the courts, the government, he said, have no say in a wife's life or behavior. Just the husband.

The woman was arrested in Portage County for breast-feeding her child while driving on the Ohio Turnpike. She was blessed to be fined only $100.

But her husband is fighting the charges, planning lawsuits and claiming the government has no right to deal with his wife—only he can do that.

He said that God said so, because the husband is supposed to be the head of the house.

If that's true, a husband could send his wife out to kill someone or sell drugs, and only he could bring any sort of justice.

He could say, "Honey, I know you had a bad day. I know you didn't mean to boil the baby like a lobster. But I have to do something—no trip to the beauty shop for you this week."

What a way to run a crime wave!

Husbands, just send your wives into the streets with automatic weapons and let them bring home the bacon (and the Lexus), because the law can't touch 'em.

I can't believe I'm even writing about this, and I know God doesn't need me as his defense attorney. But I'm sick of people turning God into Silly Putty to try and fill in gaps in their own characters. I'm sick of people having a divine scapegoat ready, as in this breast-feeding fiasco.

I wish people would stop blaming God for their own stupid decisions or using God to advance their own selfish agendas.

Somehow, I just don't think God would approve of a mother breast-feeding her child as she roars down the highway. This woman was charged with driving without a license, violating the child safety-seat laws and obstructing official business.

All the woman had to do was stop, nurse the child and then get back on the road. Isn't that why they make rest stops?

But the husband reportedly said that his wife, "didn't want to turn a five-hour trip to Michigan into a seven-hour trip."

So she nursed as she drove.

Why not say, "Michigan is so far, I don't want to spend all day on the road, so I'll drive 110 mph. And only my husband can stop me! If you don't like it, too bad. It's God's will."

I don't think any of this is God's will.

Didn't Jesus say that it's better to have a rock tied to your neck and be tossed into the ocean than to harm "one of my little ones?" Shouldn't a mother simply make time to feed a child?

Isn't this just lunacy?

More importantly, just keep God out of all this.

The husband said arresting his wife and cutting her a sweetheart deal for $100 was "bearing false witness," and therefore she couldn't get into heaven.

Don't even ask why.

I don't know and I don't care.

He also mumbled something about "freedom of religion."

What any of this has to do with breast-feeding is beyond me.

Freedom of religion is being used as a reason to legally blow dope, to oppress women, to own slaves and to not pay taxes.

So often, freedom of religion is really someone's attempt to have freedom from basic human responsibility, and I don't think any people of real faith can buy into that.

Saturday, June 28, 2003

You've seen them.

So-called "people of God," who seem to float through the world in La-La Land. Nothing bothers them. Their mood never changes. They usually smile, albeit a bit vacantly.

And they make the rest of us think we ought to do the same, at least if we love the Lord.

"There's this huge misconception that Christians are not supposed to admit they are angry," said Dr. Richard Dobbins, founder of Akron's Emerge Ministries, a Christian counseling service.

But that also goes for Jews and anyone else who claims to have a relationship with God.

Someone cuts you off in traffic . . .

Someone stabs you in the back at work . . .

Someone drops a layoff notice or divorce papers on you . . .

And you're what? Supposed to just take a deep breath and pretend it never happened?

"Too many people think so," Dobbins said. "Their body is telling them something else. Muscles are tensing. They feel flushed. There is an edge to their voice."

But whatever you do, don't admit you're angry.

That just makes it worse, right?

No, it just makes you worse, said Dr. Gary Oliver, who works at the Center for Marriage and Family Studies at John Brown University. He recently conducted a men's seminar at The Chapel.

"Anger is a secondary emotion," he told the men. "It comes from the pain of something that happened in the past, the frustration with something happening now, or the fear of what will happen in the future."

People misunderstand their anger, because they don't look at the source, Oliver said.

When they bury those emotions, they bury the emotions alive, and the emotions will come back, he said.

So they lash out at others, punch walls, withdraw into a shell, turn very sarcastic or just blame themselves by saying, "I'm just so stupid!"

And the anger really doesn't go away.

The Bible has plenty to say about anger.

In Ephesians, Paul wrote, "In your anger, do not sin."

So it's not always a sin to be angry.

"Do not let the sun go down on your anger," Paul also wrote.

Psychologists would call that confronting what makes you angry, be it a person or an event, and then trying to deal with it. It was true thousands of years ago, and nothing has changed today.

"Yet, I still see so many who are ready to explode about something that happened to them, but won't admit it," Dobbins said. "At least 70 percent of our clients have anger problems, because anger often is at the root of depression."

People tell friends what has upset them. Or they sit and stew, making mental lists of how they plan to get even.

"A fool gives full vent to his anger, but a wise man keeps himself under control," says the book of Proverbs.

Some read this and "want peace at all cost," Oliver said. They are "cream puffs," and they absorb the unfair outburst of a friend or relative because they don't want to start a fight. They equate being a punching bag (be it verbal, or even physical) with honoring God, and that's just not the case.

Being in full control of your anger means knowing you're angry and then trying to figure out why. Not just breaking things and swearing and screaming at innocent bystanders.

"Most studies now show that type of explosive behavior gives some immediate release, but in the long run, it doesn't deal with the anger," Dobbins said. "The problem is still there, and you made it worse with the destruction."

Sometimes, you can't confront the source of your anger.

You were abused or abandoned as a child. The person who did you wrong is dead. But your pain is more alive than ever.

In both the Old and New Testaments, you read that "Vengeance is mine, says the Lord."

The experts say that sometimes we just have to trust God— sort of what goes around, comes around—although they don't put it in those terms. God is the ultimate judge and jury. He sees everything. By forgiving someone who is long gone, we don't let them off the hook, we turn them over to the Lord for His judgment. There are some things that may never be explained— we just have to accept that and move on.

"Prayer often is the answer," Dobbins said. "No matter what happens, God is not angry with you. His love is greater than anything, including your anger. We just have to trust in that."

Saturday, February 17, 2001

The Truth About Some Liars

They lied.

Why can't they just admit it?

They lied because it was easier than telling the truth. They lied to get ahead. They lied because they wanted to.

I'm talking about the people in my profession, those writers who have been blatantly making up stories for profit.

Not just Jayson Blair, late of the *New York Times*.

He's just the most recent example, and about half of his last 70-some stories either had total fabrications and/or were stolen from other writers and newspapers.

Why did he do it?

Actually, I don't care why Blair or any of those other writers did it.

The *why* question doesn't matter to me. I don't even care *how* they did it. I just know these people ripped off the reading public, and they did the same to the publications that paid their salaries.

And they don't seem to get it.

Those basic commandments about Not Stealing and Not Lying—two of the Top 10—were simply ignored.

Stephen Glass fabricated details in more than 20 stories he wrote for the *New Republic* and other magazines in the late 1990s.

"I lied for self-esteem," he said.

Glass told this to "60 Minutes," five years after he was exposed. He finally made his first public apology.

Why now?

Because Glass has just published a novel about a writer who

makes up stories—and he supposedly received an advance of more than $100,000 to write it.

This makes it sick.

This guy wrote a story about an evangelical church that worshipped George Bush, father of the current president. It was not satire. He passed it off as fact. It was as phony as the story he did about a prominent black leader who supposedly had a thing for young women.

He made up nameless sources, then made up notes and voice messages and e-mails to back up his phony stories.

Why is he apologizing only now?

"Because I was ashamed," he told "60 Minutes."

No, because he's trying to sell a book.

The Blair case received far more public attention.

He said something about having "to kill Jayson Blair the journalist, so Jayson Blair the human being can live."

Spare me the self-absorbed drama.

Blair revealed this and much more in a long interview with a weekly called the *New York Observer*. He seemed to take pride in how he concocted details of the Palestine, W.Va., hometown of captured soldier Jessica Lynch. He wrote that Lynch's father stared at a tobacco field from his front porch, and that the father fought back the tears.

Never happened.

Blair never even went to the town, although the story was supposedly written from there.

He laughed about it, writer Sridhar Pappu said.

I gagged.

A father didn't know if his daughter would live, and a writer just made up a story, and now he thinks it's funny.

Blair also is working on a book and believes he'll strike it rich. Maybe he will.

As he said in the interview, "If [the *New York Times*] is so brilliant and I'm such an affirmative-action hire, how come they didn't catch me?"

It doesn't sound like Blair has been humbled by his exposure as a fraud, does it?

Know why people lie and lie and lie?

Because they are arrogant.

They believe they can get away with it simply because they are the ones saying it.

Blair also blamed race for his problems with the truth, saying the *Times* newsroom was not an easy place for minorities.

But Glass wrote all the lies he could fit into print, and he's white.

This is not an issue of color; it's about character.

Remember Janet Cooke, who won a Pulitzer Prize in 1981 for a *Washington Post* story about an eight-year-old heroin addict?

Never happened, either.

Now she is back, combining with another writer on a screenplay about her life that recently was sold to Hollywood for $750,000, according to the *Los Angeles Times*. If the movie about her actually is made, there will be another $850,000 paid.

A novelist named Lawrence Block wrote a book *Telling Lies for Fun and Profit*. But it was about how to write fiction.

People such as Blair and Glass and Cooke write lies as fact, and then get rewarded after embarrassing the people who trusted them to tell the truth.

Proverbs 19:22 reads, "Better to be poor than a liar."

Guess what?

That really is the truth.

Saturday, May 24, 2003

Can Honesty Be the Best Policy for the Bottom Line?

Imagine a crime ring that broke into 100,000 homes and stole all the cash in the drawers, then headed to the bank and emptied out all the retirement accounts.

Did it over and over and over.

Did it and lied about it.

Did it, got caught, and had no intention of paying anything back.

That's what the corporate scandals at Enron, Arthur Andersen and WorldCom are like, according to Rabbi Arthur Lavinsky of Beth El Congregation.

"Let's call it what it really is—stealing," he said. "It's pure greed, people giving in to their basest desires."

They left victims across the country, victims who had invested in those companies, who had believed the CEOs and the accountants who verified their financial statements. The corrupt executives then sent Wall Street skidding, with stocks of companies not under investigation falling simply because no one knows where the next outbreak of corruption might appear.

So many working people who have IRAs and other retirement accounts are watching their savings disappear. Directly or indirectly, many people feel as if they have been robbed.

"This is what happens when you say that you don't care about someone's character, all you care about is if they can do the job," said the Rev. Joey Johnson, pastor of the House of the Lord. "But your character has a lot to do with how you do your job."

Remember the movie *Wall Street*, in which Michael Douglas gives the "Greed is good" speech and the audience gives the corporate raider a standing ovation? That was supposed to reflect the mood of the 1980s, when insider trading was the con job of the decade.

Now, they cook the books, shred documents, and tell employees to buy stocks while executives secretly sell them. They are as heartless as someone who tosses an elderly woman out of a wheelchair and then runs off with her purse while she's left on the concrete, helpless.

Odds are, the street thug will do far more prison time than the guy who ripped off millions. Where is the justice in that?

Why do these mega-rich executives even try such boldly corrupt schemes?

"It became a case where enough was never enough," said Steve Hallam, dean of the University of Akron's business school. "It's about getting the biggest yacht, the finest wines, the largest houses. There is no limit to the hunger."

Or to the means some people will go to feed it.

"We have an addiction to a quick fix," said David Loar, pastor of Fairlawn West United Church of Christ. "Many people believe that money is the ultimate desire, even more than fame and sex."

We want what we want, and we want it now.

How often have you heard someone say, "Hey, whatever works, right?"

And we agree.

But just because it works doesn't necessarily make it right. Insider trading and lying on profit statements worked great for some executives, but cheated those who could least afford to take a financial hit.

In a *Wall Street Journal* story, an 88-year-old accountant named Al Bows told of working with Arthur Andersen, the accountant who founded the firm 88 years ago.

"He would be disgusted with what these guys did to his company," Bows said. "Most of the original [employees] are dying. It's sad. But at least they didn't have to live to see this."

President George W. Bush recently said, "There is no capitalism without conscience, no wealth without character."

But for so many years, so many people defied that and seemingly got away with it—and that holds true in politics, not just business.

The sad thing is that in certain business situations, don't we expect people to lie to us? And maybe we find ourselves stretching things, too, just because "that's how business is done."

Sometimes, we're like little kids who spill something on the floor, then look into our parents' eyes and deny we did it—even though our clothes are splattered with grape juice. Or we see something and immediately scream, "MINE! MINE!"

Ever notice how we have to teach little kids to share, but how being selfish comes naturally? And how some people never grow out of it?

"We don't have a [stock] crisis, we have a values crisis," said Johnson, of the House of the Lord. "It's only showing up in business now, but it began in the family, carried over to government and business."

Johnson said the real starting point for any discussion of ethics must be at home.

If there's no foundation there, don't expect ethical behavior anywhere else.

"We can't put our lives in compartments," said The Chapel's Knute Larson. "I'm sure some [of the executives] had spiritual lives, but they just ignored it because they didn't see how it carried over to business."

Now, we do.

For years at UA, Hallam has been teaching a business leadership graduate course that involved a serious discussion of ethics.

Now, he said, that will be even more of a focus.

"I'm encouraged because the students today seem less materialistic than those I had 20 to 25 years ago," he said. "The best thing to come out of the scandals is everyone is talking about ethics."

And it's about time.

Saturday, July 20, 2002

Let's tell the truth—we all lie.

But why do we lie when we know there's a very good chance we'll get caught? Why do we let others lie for us, knowing they'll probably be exposed?

We can ask why we ever lie, but, if we're honest, we know the answer to that question.

Because we're scared.

Because we want to spare pain, to ourselves or someone else.

Because we don't want to pay the bill for our mistakes.

Consider the case of Rep. Gary Condit, D-Calif., who spent weeks denying that he had a sexual relationship with Chandra Levy, the Washington intern who is missing.

The congressman also had members of his staff do the same, and they probably assumed their boss was telling the truth.

Only, he wasn't.

So his lie made liars out of them.

Former President Bill Clinton went through much of the same gymnastics with the truth when it came to his relationship with Monica Lewinsky.

Republicans did their share of lying in the Watergate case, in which it seemed that no one was capable of telling anything resembling the truth until John Dean began spilling the dirty secrets. And some people accused Dean of lying, or maybe of only telling the truth to save his hide.

"It has reached the point where you're kind of surprised when someone tells you the whole truth," said the Rev. Joe Kraker of St. Vincent's Catholic Church in Akron.

Several spiritual leaders said lying starts when we lie to ourselves.

"Self-deception is very strong," said the Rev. Richard McCandless of St. Paul Episcopal Church in Akron. "As somebody said, 'Denial isn't just a river in Egypt.' We lie to delay pain. We lie to buy time, hoping someone or something will save us."

One theory is that Condit thought the intern would show up in a few days and everything would be forgotten. So why bring up something that would needlessly embarrass himself, his family and the woman?

Only now more than two months have passed, and she's still missing.

And the lies have been exposed.

Lying is as old as time, Kraker said.

It began with Adam and Eve in the Garden of Eden. Satan lied to Eve, and it wasn't long before Adam and Eve were hiding from God, lying to God and lying to themselves.

The Bible says Satan is "the father of all lies."

"Abraham lied, claiming his wife was his sister," McCandless said. "Peter denied three times that he knew Jesus. They were frightened. Who hasn't been in a situation like that?"

In the case of Peter, he lied to a seemingly helpless teen-age girl, who said she saw him with Jesus.

"When we get caught in a lie, the temptation is to keep insisting we're telling the truth, and Peter began swearing to prove his point," said the Rev. Bud Olszewski of Rittman's Grace Brethren Church.

But after a while, doesn't all the lying wear you out?

"When you are in any sort of financial negotiation," Olszewski said, "you pretty much expect to be lied to and for someone to try to cheat you."

So true.

There is a scene in the movie *A Few Good Men* where Jack

Nicholson screams, "TRUTH, you want the TRUTH? You can't HANDLE the truth!"

That may be why some of us lie, why some families have deep, terrible secrets. They don't think others can deal with the truth.

"I also think people want to put off the day of reckoning," said the Rev. George Murphy of Trinity Lutheran Seminary, who also is on the staff at St. Paul's Episcopal Church.

It's known as "muddying the waters." Don't answer anything directly, confuse all you can with half-truths until no one is sure what happens, and maybe the problem will disappear.

"We live in an age where there no longer is absolute truth," said the Rev. Bill Cunningham of Medina's First Baptist Church. "Nothing is black and white. Everything is shades of gray. If you say you know the absolute truth, you're considered intolerant."

That's why you nearly pass out when someone says, "Hey, it's my fault. I messed up." And why most of us are quick to grant forgiveness to those people, assuming the apology is sincere.

"Every day, we have a choice [in how we react to things]," Cunningham said. "We can deceive ourselves. That leads to the choice to lie, and that leads to some horrible consequences. If you decide to tell the truth, that leads to good choices."

That still can lead to some very bad consequences.

But, at least, they are honest ones.

Saturday, July 14, 2001

Money makes liars of us all.

Or at least most of us.

Or at least I have to confess that there have been times when I've implied that I have more money than I really do.

Or hinted that I have less.

Or I've said, "Money doesn't matter," when it mattered.

A lot.

The subject of money comes up whenever a major athlete leaves Cleveland for more cash elsewhere, as was the case with the Tribe's Jim Thome, who signed a six-year, $85 million contract with the Philadelphia Phillies. Several people who know Thome told me, "Jimmy really wanted to sign with the Indians, but . . ."

But there was $25 million more in Philadelphia.

At the news conference announcing his signing, Thome said twice that he wanted to retire with the Tribe.

But there he was, in Philadelphia.

He said he wanted six years guaranteed, and the Indians would give him only five. Later, he said Philadelphia had a better chance to win than Cleveland. Even later, he said Philadelphia made him feel more wanted than the Indians.

Thome did what so many of us do: he took the money, and then insisted it really wasn't about money. He then looked for things that had nothing to do with money, rationalizing so we would think it wasn't about money.

When everyone knows it was all about money.

Many years ago, I agreed to ghostwrite a book that was nothing more than a spin job because my cut was $40,000, which was my biggest payday as an author. Then I made up bogus reasons for doing the book, just so I wouldn't feel like a sellout.

But I sold out, and it was my worst experience as an author. Not only that, but I just lied about this money. It was closer to $30,000, after I paid my agent's fee and expenses.

The biblical Book of Hebrews says: "Keep your life free from the love of money, and be content with what you have."

We say stuff like that all the time, because we think we should.

I recently heard a pastor say, "In most cases, people do *exactly* what they want to do."

That's so true.

Many times, I'll say, "I really wanted to be there, but . . ."

But I wasn't.

And many times, I really didn't want to be there. At least not as much as I wanted to be where I ended up. Only I don't want to say that.

Just as most of us really like money, most would rather drink Drano than admit it.

Know why Jim Thome signed with Philadelphia?

Because he wanted to.

That's the bottom line. Far fewer fans would have criticized Thome or other athletes if they had just said, "Hey, that's a big pile of cash, and I'd be an idiot to pass it up."

Even if you don't agree with the philosophy, you can respect the honesty.

But Jesus insisted, "You can't serve two masters . . . you cannot serve both God and money."

The amazing thing is that some really do follow that lead.

In pro sports, it's called the hometown discount. An athlete supposedly takes a little less to play for his current team. But we are talking mega-millions here. I had several people tell me they didn't blame Thome for leaving because "he just wanted security for his family."

Excuse me?

He wouldn't have security on a $60 million deal with the Tribe, but he does with $85 million in Philadelphia?

Doesn't money make us say silly things?

The Book of Proverbs says: "The faithful man will be richly blessed, but one eager to get rich will not go unpunished."

Many people are faithful. Many have granted their own hometown discounts by passing up lucrative job transfers to another city because of family concerns. Or not taking a promotion because it required too much travel.

They may regret it on payday, but most of the time, the rewards at home make up for it.

We don't hear these stories enough. In fact, when some people say they put the brakes on their career to stay at home with the kids or be in town more often, they almost seem to be embarrassed.

Instead, they should be proud. They should be praised. They should be held up as role models, not made to feel inadequate because they really did put their families first.

Jesus had a point when, according to the Gospel of Luke, he said: "What good is it if you gain the whole world but lose your soul?"

Or lose your family.

Many of us have seen the bumper sticker: He who dies with the most toys wins.

Actually, he who dies with the most toys is dead, just like every other corpse. And you can't take it with you, even if you are buried in a Lexus.

TOUGH TIMES

Where Is God When People Die?

Where is God among the rubble and bodies?

Where is God in the tears, the blood, the agony?

Where is God when innocent people die, when it seems the world no longer makes sense?

Are you asking any of these questions today? Even if your faith is steel, when you put it in a searing fire, it bends.

And questions gnaw away at the edges of your soul, questions about terrorists hijacking commercial jets and crashing them into buildings, killing thousands, wounding even more.

Is this a part of God's plan?

"We are in a war, but not the kind of war people think," said the Rev. Bob Combs of Norton's Grace Church. "It's a spiritual war that goes directly to the darkness of men's hearts. Think about it. Some of these terrorists were so full of hate, they were willing to die for it."

And take thousands with them.

"I can't explain God," said the Rev. Ronald Fowler of Arlington Church of God. "I just know what we have been living in is a false sense of security. In our comfort and luxury, we forget about all the insanity out there, all the innocent people who are victimized all over the world."

Or as Rabbi Arthur Lavinsky of Beth El Congregation said, "We have just had a taste of pure evil that the Middle East has been experiencing for so long. It's so evil, it defies our understanding. It's a complete assault on the values of Western civilization."

We can ask why, but do we really expect an answer? Is there an answer?

The Chapel's Knute Larson recently presented a sermon about why there is evil. Larson said the Bible tells us that we live in a fallen world dating to Adam and Eve's original sin in the Garden of Eden. He contends bad things happen to good people because there are a lot of bad people out there with God-given free will.

And they are free to do horrible things.

"The tendency will be to blame God," said Larson. "But God wants us to freely love Him, so He gave us the freedom to choose light or darkness. This shows how far we have moved from God, how we have come to totally devalue human life. It shows the need we all have for a savior."

Or as Lavinsky said, "God does not precipitate this. Those who scream 'God is great!' before they commit one of these acts go against everything God stands for."

That may be true, but what do you say to the children who lost their parents?

To the husbands whose wives were killed while sitting in front of their computers at the World Trade Center?

To the wives who kissed their husbands goodbye after dropping them off at the airport, and now will never feel their warm embrace again?

"When something like this happens, God weeps," said Fowler. "That is what we should do. Weep with those who weep, mourn with those who mourn."

At times like these, the Bible says all of creation groans.

"One of the messages from this is how tomorrow is promised to no one because our lives are so uncertain," said Combs.

Suddenly, people begin to pray, even those who aren't sure what they believe. They pray because what else is there to do? They pray even if their prayer is, "God, where are you in all of this? Are you paying attention right now? Do you have any idea what just happened? Do you?"

At times like these, creation does groan.

At times like these, we may find it impossible to pray.

At times, Fowler said we need to trust God, because what are the other options?

"Jesus said blessed are those who mourn," explained Fowler. "We often forget that until something like this happens."

Wednesday, September 12, 2001

The Blame Game Backfires

Is this what comes next, the blame game?

Jerry Falwell saying the United States "got what it deserved" because of the American Civil Liberties Union, feminists, lesbians, People for the American Way and other liberal groups?

He added: "I point the finger in their face and say you helped this happen."

Falwell later sort of apologized for his remarks, grabbing the rusty old armor of "it was taken out of context." If you read the transcript, you discover that Falwell put both feet firmly down his throat on Pat Robertson's "The 700 Club." That's why Robertson has since distanced himself, issuing a statement that Falwell's opinions are just that—Falwell's. Leave me out of it, Robertson said.

Both TV evangelists wandered into a spiritual minefield last week when they discussed what was God's will in the terrorist attacks. Were the attacks punishment for sin? Did God allow thousands to die just to wake us up, to bring us to prayer and repentance?

Falwell viewed the tragedy as an example of the wrath of God, seen in the Old Testament, where nations were destroyed for turning away from the Almighty. Most priests, ministers and rabbis believe God gives us the right to choose how we will act. Since we live in a fallen world, we end up with people making selfish, destructive decisions.

And innocent bystanders suffer for it.

You can prayerfully sort out the theological issues for yourself.

But there also was a political element in Falwell's remarks.

Notice the "sinners" singled out by him. All would be considered to the Left, and chastising them only increased Falwell's support among those who already are in his corner. Compare that to a true call for repentance, which demands that all of us search our hearts and deal with the problems in our families, our nation.

Why wouldn't Falwell talk about the soaring divorce rate, which is as high in the "church" as in general society, according to several surveys.

How about gossip? Lying? Slander? Fathers walking out on their children?

What about families who claim that God is at the center of their lives, but virtually ignore the needs of the poor? There's Internet pornography, which haunts so many men, including a surprising number who stand in the pulpits each weekend. Those are real hot-button issues that a politician/TV preacher such as Falwell dares not push, fearing the backlash.

A true prophet often isn't accepted in his hometown, and those words were spoken by Jesus in the Bible. Old Testament figures such as Jeremiah, Isaiah and even Moses saw their own people turn against them when their message cut too close to the heart.

Falwell is not alone.

Remember how some liberals took the Oklahoma City bombing masterminded by Timothy McVeigh as a chance to drop a blanket of criticism over anyone who claimed to be born again? They were said to be right-wing, Bible-toting nut cases.

Now we have some people throwing bleach in the eyes of Muslims, driving a truck into the walls of mosques, insulting anyone from the Middle East.

Somebody has to pay for the World Trade Towers, right?

For the most part, the tragedy has brought out the best in most Americans. Isn't it gratifying when police and firefighters finally receive some respect? Doesn't it make you feel good to see how people have suddenly discovered an extra reserve of patience and decency? How about the dramatic increase in church attendance and spiritual discussions?

For the country to continue this growth together, we all have to confront our own sins and prejudices individually. Jesus talked about how we can see a speck of wood in another's eye, and we miss the block of wood in our own.

Good advice.

Saturday, September 22, 2001

Everyday Life is Full of Temptation

Ever been tempted?

Had that sudden urge to tell a lie? Made some personal long-distance calls on the company phone, done some creative writing on the expense account?

How about wanting to bury someone in gossip?

Tempted?

Maybe you don't have these problems. Maybe your thoughts and motives are pure. Maybe you are able to stay above it all.

But I doubt it.

I'm just glad a transcript of my thoughts for any given day is never made public. I won't get specific, because some of my thoughts even scare me.

Dare I mention my duels with envy, anger and lust?

Not in this family newspaper.

Tempted?

For me, it's only when I'm awake.

Wait a minute, I've had some dreams . . .

Never mind.

Tempted?

There are days when I want to tell my bosses exactly where they can stick this job, and, in my mind, I do it with glee. Then I turn myself into journalism's Joan of Arc. They're burning me at the stake, and all I want to do is serve God—and be the great guy that I know I am.

Most of the time, I like my bosses. I'm not even tempted to lie about that, because it's true.

Yet, I'm tempted by self-pity.

That's an easy place to visit. Give me a little information about you, your salary, your family—and in five minutes, I can convince you that you're getting a raw deal.

Most of us don't think life is being fair to us—or at least we're sure that someone else is getting more than us. It's so tempting to play the comparison game.

Ever notice how when we keep score, we always win?

In the courts of our mind, we always sway the judge and jury to give us the verdict we want. We stack the evidence, dismiss any objections that would sidetrack our case.

Most people don't like to hear that perpetual victimhood is neither godly nor healthy, because it's so tempting to live in that psychological neighborhood.

Tempted?

Only every day, and many of us feel guilty about it.

I know people who have walked away from booze, crack, heroin and pornography. They are people of faith, yet they see themselves as sinners just because they wake up in the morning tasting Jim Beam, or longing for a whiff of marijuana.

I know of people who fell away from their marriage, then returned. They'll tell you how God has healed the relationship, and it's been good for a long time.

Then they will catch a glimpse of something that reminds them of that other person, and they'll remember the good parts of that destructive time.

They'll fight it off.

But they've been tempted, and even though they survived, the spiritual battle was so fierce, they ended up feeling like sinners.

We all should know that temptation is not sin, that everyone is tempted. Christians can tell you how Jesus was attacked with three major temptations, one after another, like tidal waves pounding the shore.

But we keep it a secret, as if temptation was a sign of weakness rather than a fact of everyday life.

How many of us have a friend we can call when we're in that moral swamp, and feel ourselves sinking? How many of us pray at these times? How many of us know we need help, but are afraid to ask? How many of us have prayed for God to send us someone to stand next to us in these wars?

Temptation often becomes sin when we try to go it alone. This is where friends need to pray with each other, to lift up and celebrate when temptations are defeated. But to do that, we have to risk being honest—with ourselves, and someone else.

Saturday, September 20, 2003

The Colossal Courage of Hal McCoy

Some days you think it's back, mornings when you wake up and you can almost see the world again.

There are moments when things look normal . . . almost.

But you know better.

Think of the death of a spouse. You can almost hear him in the other room, sniff a trace of him lingering in the air.

For a few minutes, you feel the grief fading.

But you know better.

You look in the mirror at your eyes, to see if there has been some type of miracle . . .

But you know better.

You can't even see the color of your own eyes.

You're Hal McCoy.

You're 62 years old. You're going to be inducted today into the writers wing of the Baseball Hall of Fame, "the Pulitzer Prize of baseball," you call it.

You think about growing up in Akron, about those first six years living in Lakemore, almost a shack on stilts near the water. You played catch with your dad, the outhouse serving as a backstop.

That's right, the outhouse . . .

The outside pump for drinking water . . .

The bucket of bolts that was the car, where you could glance down at the holes in the floor and see the concrete street below. You often rode down Front Street, which was nothing but dirt, holes, loose stones.

You've come a long way . . . you're Hal McCoy.

You played first base at East High. You could hold up your glove, close your eyes and not have to worry when the ball was hit to Gene Michael, your shortstop. Each of his throws was perfect, landing right where you held your glove. No wonder he became a shortstop with the New York Yankees.

With Michael, you could almost play the game blindfolded. And that's how you sometimes feel when you write about baseball today for the *Dayton Daily News*.

They have ruled you as "legally blind."

You've had strokes in both eyes, the latest on January 23. It was a morning when you awoke and your world was gone. Not black. Just fuzzy. Just blurry. Just hazy.

You squinted. You rubbed your eyes. You put on your glasses. You took off your glasses and cleaned them, rubbed the lenses furiously. You put them back on. Everything was so dark, so vague, it was like living inside a cloud.

That's how it still is today.

You see, but you don't.

You see shades, but not colors.

You see food on your plate, but you're not always sure what it is. Peas? Corn? Something round, but what?

You see words on your enlarged computer screen sharply some days, other times it appears the letters are wavy, under water.

You love to read, and sometimes when the lighting is just right, you can. Reading glasses are all you need. Other days, you don't see the words on the edges of the page, sentences just end in the middle.

You can't drive. The last time you tried, you wrecked your car and were thankful you didn't kill yourself or someone else. Humbled and angry that you'd never be able to drive again, you have to ask someone to chauffeur you around. You've become an imposition, and you hate that.

From day to day, you still don't know what you'll see.

But you don't need 20-20 vision to feel how people love you, or to learn the true value of patience, prayer and kindness.

You won't say that this has been the best thing that has ever happened to you, but it's not the worst.

You're Hal McCoy.

For the past 31 years, your job has been reporting on the Cincinnati Reds. This spring, you were ready to quit. This spring, you arrived at the Sarasota, Fla., airport and couldn't find your luggage. The suitcases were the same ones you've had for the past five years. They were on the carousel, going around and around and around.

You couldn't tell them from the other bags . . .

Until there were no other bags left.

On that first day of spring training, you arrived at the Reds' clubhouse and you couldn't tell one player from another. You sat on a chair. You tried not to cry. Third baseman Aaron Boone came up to you, started talking about your selection to the Hall of Fame . . .

When you were a little kid living on Seiberling Street in Akron, you played games with baseball cards. Then you wrote up the imaginary games, put a headline on it. Created your own sports page.

You were 10.

You used to sneak into the Goodyear Gym to see the Wingfoots play basketball. You'd wait until the *Beacon Journal* sportswriter would finish writing, then you'd grab his story written on Western Union paper.

You had a business teacher named Rose Paolucci who also was the moderator of the East High Caravan. When you played on the basketball team, she convinced you to write about the games for the school paper. You did. You loved it. You had a calling.

Ever since you could remember, all you ever wanted to be was a sports writer.

You were the sports editor of the *Daily Kent Stater*. You paid dues covering high schools, colleges, sports that barely were a blip on most journalistic radar screens.

In spring training with Aaron Boone listening to your story, it wasn't just about the Hall of Fame.

You couldn't see.

Not just because of the damage to your eyes, but the tears. The fear. The sinking feeling gnawing away at your gut that your life as you knew it was over.

You were a baseball writer.

That's what you started to tell Aaron Boone, but he wouldn't hear it.

"You can't quit," he said.

You stared at him.

"You can't quit," he insisted. "You're not a quitter. We'll help you."

And so many people have done just that. Even now, as you think of it, the tears come back.

Tears of gratitude.

You're Hal McCoy.

Six times you've been honored as the Ohio Sportswriter of the Year. You've written two books and are working on one with Reds first baseman Sean Casey.

But that doesn't mean much now, at least compared with what you've been hearing lately.

You're humbled when Reds Manager Bob Boone says, "Hal is fair. He'll rip me and my team, but he's still fair about it. I like people with character, and Hal has character. He can play on my team."

You don't know what to say when pitcher Danny Graves confides, "He treats you as a person. He cares about you. He has a way of criticizing you, but he doesn't put you down."

You love it when the players kid you, "Hey, Hal, they say if you watch too many dirty movies, you go blind. Is that true?"

You relish the locker room talk. You ask Graves how he gets through airport metal detectors with all his body piercing. The pitcher laughs, pulls up his shirt and shows you his nipple rings and the stud in his navel.

You take it as the ultimate compliment when Casey says, "Unless you knew it, you'd never guess Hal has a problem with his vision."

You have learned to compensate. You can see body shapes. You find your hearing is sharper than ever. You learn to count steps. You walk slowly, almost a trudge. You know if you really concentrate, and look down, you usually won't trip. Your wife marks your bags with a big, white bow, because you usually can pick that out in your dark world.

You're Hal McCoy.

You always thought you were so strong, so self-sufficient, able to take care of not just yourself, but others.

Then comes the day you packed your bags, opened your hotel room door and walked straight into the closet, banging your head on a rack of hangers.

And the day you fell on the escalator in the Denver airport, ripping your jeans, cutting your knee, and even worse, bruising your ego.

And the day you gashed your head on the top of a car trunk, reaching in to grab a suitcase. You never saw it until it felt like someone took a sledgehammer to your skull and the blood flowed.

And then there are conversations with Coke machines you thought were people, or people you thought were standing there—only they're gone.

Most of the time, you've been able to shrug it off, often with a grin, thinking this will make a good story to tell your wife. But those nights when you can't sleep, when you think back on the frustrations of the day, you never saw this coming.

Life in the dark.

You're Hal McCoy.

Your wife is the reason you're still in the press box. Nadine is the one who lets you cry in her arms, who holds you tight, then says, "Remember, you can still do the job you love, how many people can ever say that?"

How many indeed?

Not your father, Harold, who worked more than 50 years for B.F. Goodrich.

Not your recently deceased mother, Hazel, who worked at a laundry.

Not when you were growing up and worked an A&W root beer stand near the Rubber Bowl or when you cooked french fries at the Waterloo Drive-In.

Then your wife said something else.

"You think you're going to quit, what are you going to do, just sit around and feel sorry for yourself?" Nadine said. "I'm not going to have that."

You have a sports editor named Frank Corsoe.

You approached Frank with the medical reports on your eyes. It was a nightmare. Most of the vision was gone, and not about to come back. Doctors were out of ideas. You'd have to live with it.

You offered to resign.

Corsoe would eat broken glass before he'd let you quit.

He said, "OK, you can't drive. But we'll get you a ride. We'll get you the help you need. Let's try it."

Every day, an intern picks you up at the house, drives you to the park. On the road, writers from other papers help.

You still write about 20 stories each week. You still have yet to miss a baseball trip in 31 years. You average 155 games per season. You have no plans to change that.

You might not see the balls hit to the outfield, but you have a TV right next to you in the press box, and you have learned to follow the action, to watch baseball through muddy water.

You sometimes need twice as long to write your stories. Your eyes get tired and just sort of shut down for 5 to 10 minutes. You still try to rub those glasses clean, as if that will help. You still squint, as if that will help. You still stumble on stairs, struggle in dimly lit restaurants, become angry because you can't drive and have to rely on others.

You used to play tennis at least five times a week, at 6 a.m.

Not now.

That's gone, too.

You're Hal McCoy.

You wish you had your sight back, just for a moment.

You want to see your wife's face, those green eyes that are nothing more than a memory to you now.

But just when you think it's not worth it, someone will call. A fellow writer, a friend, a player. Then there are the fans. The e-mails, more than a thousand of them. One from a guy on an aircraft carrier near Iraq. He tells you not to quit. He says he's praying for you. You can't believe a guy in a war zone is worried about you.

You find yourself talking to God, attending the baseball chapel. You never were much for prayer, but you sometimes drop to your knees and pray—not as much for yourself as for others who are in the midst of pain, storms and trials.

In the dark, you discover a glimpse of spiritual light.

People with sight problems say you have to keep going, that you are representing every visually impaired person. You appreciate that, but you really are doing it for yourself, because this is what you've always done.

You're Hal McCoy, Hall of Fame baseball writer, and you press on.

Sunday, July 27, 2003

Gossip: The Spark that Ignites

I'll never forget the phone call from a friend . . .

"I heard this, but I can't believe it," he said.

A juicy bit of gossip was about to come my way, and I couldn't resist. I knew I shouldn't listen, but I did.

I *wanted* to hear it.

Then, I found out it was about . . . *me*!

About how I screamed at a young writer, cussed him out in front of several people, and finished by saying, "I'm the star, and you're not, so just do what I say."

My heart sank. Nothing even close to that happened. The young writer was a friend, someone for whom I was serving as a mentor.

"You know me," I said. "You know my relationship with [the other writer]. Do you think I'd do something that like?"

The person said, "Of course not. I just thought you should know what they're saying."

"Who's saying it?" I asked.

"You know . . ."

His voice trailed off. He wasn't about to tell, and there wasn't much I could do.

The incident is nine years old, and it still stings. It should stop me from gossiping about others, but that's not always the case.

"There's something about our hearts that enjoys the pain of other people, and we often celebrate their troubles," said Dennis Butts, one of the pastors at the House of the Lord.

Butts said it's like driving down the road and seeing an accident off to the side. We know we should just keep driving, that it's none of our business, but we slow down and take a look.

"We sort of dismiss gossip," Butts said. "We say we didn't steal, we didn't murder anyone. But we can kill their reputations, and the Bible says it's a sin."

A few days ago, Jim Colledge received one of those phone calls from a friend.

"You know that Ann Graham Lotz is coming to Cleveland for a women's conference," the friend said.

Colledge, the pastor of Hudson Community Chapel, told her he was aware of that.

"I understand you have a problem with her theology," the friend said.

Colledge actually had given very little thought to Lotz—period. But suddenly he discovered that someone was saying he didn't like Lotz, who is a daughter of Billy Graham. Not a great spot for the pastor of an evangelical church to find himself in.

He wondered how he had even been dragged into anyone's discussion of Ann Graham Lotz. He couldn't remember even talking to anyone about Ann Graham Lotz.

"Gossip and rumors are so invisible, so destructive," Colledge said. "But there is something about it that makes us want to hear it, and maybe spread it. We feel better about ourselves when we hear someone else being torn down."

The business world oozes gossip. Someone always has the "real story" about why a certain deal went down, or why someone received a promotion. Seldom is the story uplifting.

When a sports team makes a major trade, I usually receive a couple of calls from fans saying a certain team "got rid of [player X] because he was having an affair with . . ."

The truth is, the guy couldn't hit anymore or wanted more money than the team was willing to pay him. The reason is often very obvious, but the obvious isn't enough for some people.

They insist there has to be some "real dirt" that I'm refusing to tell the readers.

Nor does it matter that families shatter over rumors and gossip. Churches split. Lives are ruined. We want to hear it anyway.

I once received this e-mail from a fan: "Write some more trade rumors, even if they're not true. They're fun to talk about."

Fun? Not to the guy and his family in the middle of the bogus rumor.

"When someone starts to tell me something, I ask who said it. If they won't tell me, then I refuse to listen," said Pete Drury, pastor of Valleyview Chapel in Wadsworth.

Drury also said we should be aware of when someone drops his or her voice, or wants to take us away from everyone else and whisper something in the corner. Often, those are warning signs that gossip is on the way.

There's something else about gossip. "It can be bad even if it's true," said Rabbi Arthur Lavinsky of Beth El Congregation.

Jewish tradition views gossip like murder, Lavinsky said. The person who is spoken about is damaged, and the person who does the speaking and those who listen are equally guilty.

"If you embarrass someone, we believe it is like you spilled their blood," he said. "That comes from seeing someone's face red and flushed. You are taking the life out of them."

Lavinsky told the ancient Jewish story of someone who apologized to a rabbi for spreading rumors about him.

The rabbi said it was like a man who goes to the top of a mountain, cuts open a pillow, and watches hundreds of feathers float down. To make it right, you'd have to gather up each feather, and who can do that? Who can stop the gossip?

Yet, I still gossip. I still listen to gossip. A few weeks ago, I savaged three people in a five-minute conversation. I wanted to cut my tongue later, but it was too late. I felt like the guy with the pillow and the feathers.

Lavinsky said we should all memorize Psalm 34:13: "Keep your tongue from evil and your lips from speaking lies."

I tell people that James is one of my favorite New Testament books, yet I don't follow it, especially the parts where he writes that the tongue is like a spark that sets off "a great forest fire . . . it corrupts the whole person."

Now there's a message we all should spread.

Saturday, February 2, 2002

When Bad Things Happen to Good People, There are No Answers

There is no answer.

At least there is none that most of us want when it comes to something like Stow DARE officer Tobie Cozy Reed, who is 32 years old, being consumed by cancer and given only six months to live.

Reed has spent her life trying to do the right things as a model wife, mother and officer.

Only now, doctors say that life is coming to an end.

You may have read Stephen Dyer's moving story about Reed in the *Akron Beacon Journal*. She is handling her illness with the kind of grace that only can come from God.

Yet, most of us ask, "Where is the justice in this?"

And some will ask, "Why does God want to take this woman, leaving a husband and children behind?"

It's the question of the ages: Why do bad things happen to good people?

What's the deal when 15-year-old Josh Miller dies? He was an honor student/linebacker at Barberton High School, an excellent person by all accounts.

Yet he collapsed with a heart problem and passed away on the sidelines during a football game.

Why?

Where is God in all this?

"You can't begin to understand it," said the Rev. Joseph Kraker of St. Vincent's Catholic Church.

That's not a bad way to start, because most of us are sick of simple, saccharine answers to these questions. Because we know that the words and the people saying them are phony.

"God may not seem like He's in the middle of something like cancer, but He is at the end of it," Kraker said. "Does it seem fair? No. Do I know why these things happen? No. Do I trust God, do I believe He is waiting for this woman, that He loves her? That I have no doubt."

Maybe that doesn't sound like much to you—heaven being at the end of a long road of agony.

"But that's because some people don't understand what life in eternity with God will be," said Pastor Butch Pursley of Maranatha Bible Church.

"We have this perception of God as Santa Claus. He should do what we want, and when He doesn't, we get upset. Most great men and women of God suffered incredibly. The Bible is full of stories of pain and hardship."

That's not optimistic.

"Some churches have people always looking for quick answers and quick fixes," Pursley said. "The idea being spread is, if you're faithful to God, you'll always be healthy and wealthy. That's just not true."

What happens when someone such as Reed gets cancer? Or when someone you love is killed by a drunken driver? Everyone knows of a tragedy that rips your heart out.

"God does allow certain hardship," said Pastor Keith Johnson of Redeemer Lutheran Church in Cuyahoga Falls. "I think of St. Paul, how three times he went to God about the thorn in his flesh, and three times God didn't answer his prayer. Finally, God said, 'My grace is sufficient.' I know that suffering does build character, and I know God's grace is sufficient."

All of that is true, especially if you ask yourself: Do I learn more from the good times or the bad times? Most of us grew during our ordeals. But they still hurt. And sometimes, the person doesn't survive.

As Pastor David Wilkerson of New York's Times Square Church has said, "You have every right to ask God, 'Why?' But He probably won't answer. He seldom has for me. He didn't for Job."

Wilkerson is the author of the longtime best-seller *Cross and Switchblade*. He has seen his wife endure five different kinds of cancers, and both of his daughters have had cancer. All have survived, but Wilkerson was like so many people in that situation.

You start asking, "Hey, what did I do to deserve this?"

There is no answer.

"There is just faith," said Pastor Ron Fowler of the Arlington Church of God. "There is knowing that God won't keep you from pain and death, but He will walk with you every step of the way."

Really, what choice do we have?

Do we go it alone? Or do you believe there is something after death? Do we believe that God does love us, that He does have a plan, even if we don't get it?

In the end, those are the questions we really have to answer.

Saturday, December 9, 2000

An Olympic Test of Their Faith

Olympian Mark Croghan loves to run.

Kim Croghan loves to make lists, to plan, to feel that life is under control.

Then, came the baby.

Griffin Croghan was born September 3, 1999, with a heart defect, and everything changed.

What does running matter, when the baby might die? How can you plan when tomorrow isn't guaranteed? What good are your lists when you don't know what to write down?

Especially, when you're in a hospital waiting room, a doctor in front of you. Weary. Stonefaced. His skin a gloomy gray.

You don't know the news, you just know it's bad.

The baby is on a heart/lung machine. The baby needs a heart transplant. The baby might not live to see the morning.

"Wait a minute," you say. "This isn't happening."

Yes, it was open-heart surgery on a seven-month-old boy, but the danger was supposed to have been minimal. A few snips, a little tinkering and everything would be OK. Better than new. Five days after surgery, the baby comes home.

And life is back to normal.

That's what the doctors said. That was back in June, but it's the middle of August and Griffin remains at Cleveland's Rainbow Babies and Children's Hospital.

And the Croghans now know there's no such thing as normal.

Not after Griffin.

Always smiling Griffin. Huggy, giggling Griffin. Then, there was Griffin hooked up to tubes, to machines, to something to pump blood to the heart and lungs. There was Griffin, once so full of life, staring at the ceiling, nearly comatose.

There were nights when Kim and Mark Croghan could do nothing but hold hands. Hold hands and cry.

And pray.

Those nights, their Christianity was stripped of every religious cliche, slammed against the wall of life and death—and left to see if it was real. Their five-year marriage was put on trial. Would they pull together, or break apart under the pressure?

"You can't help but ask yourself, 'Why?'" said Kim Croghan. "'Why our baby?'"

Or as grandfather Dan Croghan asked: "You tell yourself that it's not fair. Why would God bring a child into the world, only to have a baby go through all this?"

Yes, this.

This is an infant born with a heart condition.

This is an infant having an operation to correct the heart problem, only it became worse. Much worse. The baby had a stroke, could barely move his leg or arm on his right side.

This is kidney problems, vision problems, speech problems.

"There are no birth defects on either side of our family," said Kim Croghan. "Our three-year-old [Cameron] is perfectly healthy. You start to wonder if you did something wrong. Is God punishing you? Does he hate you? If so, why? That's when you have to grab on to your faith."

What's the other option? Howling at God? Demanding answers when you know there are none? So you trust something unseen, something bigger than yourself and your world, because you must.

"This has made me realize that God is in charge of things, even when I don't understand them," Croghan said.

Not that surrendering is easy.

"You just want to fix it, to make it better," said Dan Croghan.

"But you can't. My wife [Judy] spends a lot of time on the Internet, looking for information. But after a while, you have to realize, unless you're a doctor, there's not much you can do."

So the Croghans take their three-year-old swimming, to the park. They tell him that his baby brother "has a boo-boo on his heart." Cameron goes to Rainbow, plays with the other kids—those with bald heads and dying of cancer, and those full of life and making remarkable recoveries from other diseases.

They drive from their Wadsworth home to the University Hospital complex on Cleveland's East Side—every day—an hour each way.

They walk the hospital halls, they eat the hospital food, they talk the hospital talk with the hospital people.

"You learn to go day to day, because you have no other choice," Croghan said.

"That's so true," said Bob Combs, the Croghans' pastor from Grace Church. "I told them that none of us has the answers to all this. I believe there is a reason, but when you're in the middle of it, you can't see it. I know that when I get to heaven, there are some things I'd like to ask God about."

He's not alone.

The father is an Olympic steeplechase runner, a member of the U.S. team in 1992, 1996 and this year in Sydney.

The mother is a former cross-country runner at Ohio State, who still looks as if she could do three miles at a gallop without breaking a sweat.

And the baby's 18-pound body is under siege. No one is sure how well he'll be able to speak . . . to walk . . . to see.

Sometimes, the signs are good.

"The other day, he called me 'Ma-ma,'" said Kim Croghan.

But doctors still hesitate about making a long-term prognosis, because the situation has been so volatile.

"You want answers," said Dan Croghan, Mark's father,

who is also the mayor of Green. "I've never faced a problem I couldn't solve, one way or another."

But not this time. Not with Griffin.

Yes, there are truly great doctors at Rainbow Babies and Children's Hospital, where Griffin has been for three months. But twice, those doctors have told the Croghans to prepare for the worst. Twice, Griffin was placed on the heart-transplant waiting list.

"The worst was when he had the stroke," said Jeff Bogue, another pastor from Grace Church. "I was with them. Everybody was so excited, because the surgery went well, and it looked like he'd be off the heart/lung machine. Then, the next morning, they said Griffin had had a stroke."

How does a nine-month-old have a stroke? And what does it mean?

"You start to wonder if the poor thing will be a vegetable, or if he'll ever be able to walk," said Bogue. "It's so scary."

"There are times I've even planned his funeral in my head," said Kim Croghan. "What he'd wear. What I'd do with his clothes. What I'd do with his room. What I'd tell Cameron. I can't help it."

The listmaker and the planner dealing with the crisis her own way.

And her husband?

"There were a couple of days where I did nothing but blubber," Croghan said. "I was so emotional, I could hardly talk about him without crying."

"Mark has always been the emotional one in our family," said his mother, Judy Croghan. "At their wedding, Mark started crying when Kim came down the aisle. Kim didn't cry, but Mark did. Kim is the stronger one. I mean, Kim has cried during all this with Griffin, but she also has been the rock for the whole family."

The truth is, the Croghans don't know what will happen to Griffin.

Lately, the news is good. He is off the heart/lung machine, off the heart-transplant list. He still spends much of the day with a feeding tube connected to his nose, an IV in his chest.

"For a while, we'd have one good day for every three bad days," said Judy Croghan.

"Now, it's the other way around."

Through it all, Croghan is training for the Olympics. He was America's top-ranked steeplechase runner from 1992–97. He was ranked No. 2 in 1998, but dropped to No. 5 last year in the midst of an 18-month slump.

During the time Kim was pregnant with Griffin, the Croghans wondered if Mark was finished as a runner. His times had dropped drastically. He no longer had the same endurance in practice.

"I was looking into other jobs for him," said Kim Croghan. "Insurance. Real estate. We could run a day-care business. I was doing my list thing again."

Croghan simply told his wife, "I don't want to talk about it."

He kept running, kept searching, kept wondering what was wrong.

Then, doctors discovered he had an iron deficiency. Vitamins were added to his diet and, suddenly, at 32, he was running better than he had in years.

He went to the Olympic trials in Sacramento and finished second, earning a spot on the U.S. team.

"I was very relaxed," he said. "I wanted to make the team, but it wasn't life and death like before. I used to overtrain before big races, and I probably worried too much.

"With Griffin, I didn't have time for that."

Dan went with his son to Sacramento for the race, while Judy and Kim watched the trials from Griffin's hospital room.

"He was tremendous," said Dan Croghan. "In the past, Mark got himself uptight before some races, not sleeping, not eating.

I think Griffin just took the pressure off, and he really ran like he can."

Being a member of the Olympic team is critical for Croghan, because it pays for his family's health insurance.

His shoe contract with Adidas pays for most of the expenses, along with money he makes running in European meets, where track is far more popular than here.

"When I was struggling last year, Adidas could have cut me loose," Croghan said. "I'll always appreciate how they stuck by me, considering how things have gone with Griffin."

Over and over, the Croghans stress the good things that have come from Griffin's illness. Part of it is true, and part of it is a way just for them to keep going, to make the long drives, to meet with the doctors, to wait and see what an uncertain tomorrow brings.

Kim Croghan is remarkably upbeat, continually telling herself that God is at work in the midst of all this. She talks about the already close-knit families becoming even tighter, circling wagons around Griffin, taking turns baby-sitting Cameron, having people from their church support them.

"With all the prayers said for Griffin, I'm surprised he isn't just floating over the bed," said Kim Croghan.

She talks about the "super staff " at Rainbow, and how Griffin "really hasn't been in much pain, especially compared to so many other children here."

And Rainbow is a bright, cheery place.

"But you know that a baby dies there about every other day," said Dan Croghan. "Some of those kids there, it just rips your heart out to see them. I know it sounds selfish, but sometimes I don't even look in the other rooms at other kids, because I know that someone just got some bad news. I just can't handle it."

The Croghans hope that Griffin will be well enough to come home by September 3, his first birthday. Doctors say it's a possibility. The pacemaker in Griffin's heart has enabled him to get off most machines.

"If not, we'll just celebrate it at the hospital," said Kim Croghan.

"We'll make the best of what God gives us."

Sunday, August 13, 2000

Faith Can Ease Teen Angst

Another school shooting, another chorus of voices, virtually all of them from adults telling us what kids think.

But do we really know what is on the minds of young people, how they feel about Columbine, Santee and the rest?

To find out, I spent time with five seniors from Manchester High School: Carrie Toth, Brian Hill, Cristina Stone, Mike Marich and Rob Auker.

One statement they all agree on is: "When I heard about the latest shooting, my heart just broke."

Those words came from Carrie, who remembered when she was in junior high. She had two friends, a boy and a girl. The female friend dropped her, then the male friend did the same.

"You feel so alone," she said. "For a while, I stopped eating. I thought everyone was talking about me. I got to where I hated the world."

It's a big step from feeling that way to picking up a gun, but that raw emotion—"I hate the world, and the world hates me"—ate away at those who pulled the triggers at Columbine and Santee.

"There's a lot of anger, a lot of rage," Rob said. "It happens when you don't fit in. I remember back in the fifth grade, I thought about committing suicide."

That's hard to believe. Rob is an honor student, a starter on the football team, a handsome kid headed for Johnson Bible College.

"But in the fifth grade I felt fat and stupid," he said. "I had no friends, and the other kids called me a 'little porker.' It's easy to start to hate everyone when it gets like that. For me, the turning point was going to a Christian summer camp, where I got a whole new outlook on things. I didn't think everyone hated me anymore."

Carrie also said there was a change in her life when she became serious about finding a spiritual focus.

"When I was going through all that in the eighth grade, I didn't even know if there was a God," Carrie said. "I thought the Bible was a fable. My mother started taking me to church, and I thought that was dumb and boring, too. The preacher went on and on about stuff that didn't relate to me."

But Carrie joined a youth group and found kids talking about Christ, kids who accepted her. She found hope.

That's what so many kids are looking for, these students said. They want a reason to believe. Or as Carrie said, "I wanted to know why I was here."

When no answers make sense, kids drift.

"You go through a stage where you don't want to listen to anyone," Rob said. "You start to say there's nothing to do, so you booze it up. Or you have sex a lot. Or you do drugs."

Or all of the above, said Cristina, a starter on the Manchester girls basketball team.

"People have no idea what goes on at those parties," she said. "Kids think they're having a good time, but they're not. They're just sort of lost."

Cristina knows because she stepped away from the party scene a little over a year ago.

"You think you make friends that way," she said. "And you start to hate your parents. You feel like an outcast. There's just so much darkness."

So you try to party your way through it.

Cristina grew up in a home where church was considered important, but she rejected it in her early high school years. Then, she found her heart aching for something else, for that reason to go on. Carrie told her about her faith in God, about a group of Christians at the school called Solid Fog. Cristina was desperate enough to try it.

"When I quit going to parties, I lost a lot of friends," Cristina said. "I got scared. My old friends said I thought I was now too good for them, and that really hurt."

The kids at Manchester don't seem to believe a school shooting can happen there, and the horrible scenes elsewhere seem almost like a movie. But the feeling of alienation that drove those shooters is very real.

So is the tendency for those who feel that no one cares about them to join up with others who are just as angry—and to feed off each other while cutting themselves off from the rest of the school.

"The danger is that those of us who found a group can get isolated and judgmental," Rob said. "Some kids are called 'freaks,' and they dress real dirty. You talk to them and your friends say, 'What are you doing? Don't you know the stories about him or her? They have sex every night.' I want to look into their hearts and touch them, because I know they hurt."

Christian kids also find themselves ridiculed—for wearing a cross or carrying a Bible. Many of them have read various books about Columbine, especially *She Said Yes: The Unlikely Martyrdom of Cassie Bernall* by Misty Bernall, and say that gives them strength.

"When I walked away from the parties, I ended up losing about 20 friends, but I found 30 new ones when I came to the Lord," Cristina said. "I get along with my parents now. It's so great, we really trust each other. I just don't feel dark and dirty anymore. I wish every kid can feel the same way."

Saturday, March 17, 2001

New Season, Sad Memories: A Team Struggles to Make Sense of Their Sorrow

---

Ken Miller saw the children in Barberton Magics purple shirts, and his voice cracked.

"I used to bring Josh to the games when he was like that, just a little kid," he said.

He blinked several times, the tears refusing to stop.

"Josh always wanted to play for the Magics," he said. "You should see his room, full of Barberton stuff, full of Ohio State stuff. Those were his two favorite teams."

Now, that room has pictures of Josh, put up by his brothers, Ken and Justin. But the room "feels empty." Ken is "absolutely drained." His wife, Jerri, has been "crushed," according to her husband.

"My wife just couldn't be here," he said. "I'm sure she's at the cemetery. She goes there every night."

To visit Josh Miller, dead at 15.

Josh Miller, straight-A student, gritty middle linebacker, and, most important, "just a good son, a joy," according to his father.

Josh Miller's number 45 was retired before last night's game, a 10-7 victory by Wadsworth at Rudy Sharkey Stadium. The Magics also retired the jerseys of Rayshun Davis (No. 1) and Ken Sennett (No. 18), former players who also passed away.

Ken Miller was supported by his brother Jim, his son Justin and some other relatives, as he received Josh's jersey last night. It was on the same field where Josh collapsed during the final game of last season.

According to Miller, his son passed away of a "rare disease of the heart that attacks the right ventricle."

It happened on the sideline near the home grandstand. Miller had just finished talking to assistant coach Bill Adair, and he was heading for a cup of water when he went down as his parents watched.

"I have no idea how they could stand it, to see that happen to your son," Barberton coach Tim Flossie said. "I can't even look at the spot where it happened. That's why we've moved our bench to the other sidelines. It's just too much . . ."

His voice trailed off.

It was about 20 minutes before last night's game, and Flossie stared at that sideline. He thought of Miller, his inspirational leader even though he was only a sophomore last year. He thought of Rayshun Davis, another Barberton player who passed away in a drowning accident in 1999. He thought of his father, legendary coach Babe Flossie, who died this summer.

"This is the first time in 30 years I've coached a game without my dad being there," Flossie said. "He'd pace the sidelines, smoking a cigarette. He used to think that throwing one pass was too much."

Flossie thought for a moment.

"We've had two players die here in the last two years: Josh and Rayshun," he said. "I've been a coach for 30 years, but nothing has prepared me for this."

Ross and Reid Billick are twins, linemen on the Barberton team.

They moved to Barberton in the eighth grade, and one of their first friends was Josh Miller.

"He was like that," Ross Billick said. "He got me into sports. It's not right, what happened, just not right."

"He was my best friend," Reid Billick said. "I love how he played football. He played hard, so hard."

Reid Billick barely could speak, the memories too fresh, the pain too deep.

That's because Reid and Ross Billick, along with Tim Flohr, go to Greenlawn Cemetery each week.

"We talk to Josh," said Flohr, a wide receiver. "When it happened, I couldn't handle it. For about a month, I barely ate. I didn't want to talk to anyone. It's weird, I feel like he's still here, and that's why this is so hard—playing a game without him."

Ken Miller talked about Josh.

"Josh was dominating in Pee Wee football, a nose guard who no one could tackle," he said. "I still have movies of that. It was a fun time. It was pure football, not so serious."

He shook his head.

"There were no signs [of heart trouble]," he said. "Josh would go through two-a-days for football practice, and then he'd come home and run for an hour. He was never tired, never out of breath."

It's hard for anyone to imagine a kid whose spiritual heart was so huge, so vibrant—that it would just stop.

"I remember the night it happened," said Mike Gibson, a Barberton lineman. "Just a few minutes earlier, he came up to me, told me to keep my head up. He was like that, looking out for other people."

Gibson paused.

"I ask myself why that had to had to happen to Josh," Gibson said. "I ask that a million times."

The last time Barberton had a home game, it ended before the clock ticked to zero. It ended with about 2,000 people holding hands and praying as an ambulance carried Josh Miller off the field. It ended with the student section crying, chanting Josh's name, begging him to "get up, get up."

It ended later that night, hundreds of people at the Barberton Citizens Hospital, many of them on their knees, praying.

It ended, but it didn't end.

Before last night's game, Flossie told his team, "All year, we say not to play for Josh, but play like Josh. He played so hard, so doggone hard, with so much heart, it just burst."

Flossie's voice was shaky, his eyes burning with tears.

"We need to play this one for Josh, for Rayshun Davis, for my dad," he said.

The players who had been silent . . . some just pacing from one end of the room to the other . . . others who just sat silently on the floor with a blank stare . . . still others thinking about a game, and about two teammates who died when kids aren't supposed to die . . . they roared at Flossie's final words, rushed out the door, anxious to move their bodies, to do something to take away the pain.

Josh Miller was 5-foot-9 and an outstanding wrestler in addition to being a football player.

"The papers kept saying Josh was 155," Ken Miller said. "He was 179 at the autopsy. I wish people knew that."

It's strange how a father's mind works in this situation. His son had lifted so many weights, pushed himself with such determination, and his dad wanted everyone to know the sweat was paying off.

Josh was getting bigger, gaining weight, just like he wanted.

"He had a 4.56 grade-point average on his last report card," Ken Miller said. "He got all A's in his honors courses."

Ken Miller has heard people say well-intentioned thoughts, but most don't help.

"I hear that God wanted Josh with him in heaven," he said. "But God can have Josh for an eternity. I just wish that we could have had Josh for 30 years."

Ken Miller talked about losing his sister when he was only six years old.

"Hit by a car right in front of our house," he said.

About his father passing away when Ken was 15.

"Brain aneurysm," he said.

Now, Josh.

"They say God only gives you what you can handle," he said. "But this is a lot, an awful lot. It has tested my faith."

Ken Miller is 47. He has spent his entire life in Barberton. He works as a manufacturer's representative for R.R. Engine & Machine in Akron, a job he has had for the past 18 years.

He couldn't watch much of the game last night. He spent most of the evening on the grass, near the end zone, talking to relatives and friends about Josh, doing it between tears that seemed like they'd never really stop.

Left unsaid was that he should have been watching Josh, who should have been a junior, a star middle linebacker.

"I always came to these games," he said. "But now, I just don't know if I can. It just hurts so much."

Saturday, August 25, 2001

Ever face a crisis alone?

Ever call out to friends and they just don't get it? They listen, but they don't hear? Their attention fades; they tune you out.

Ever wish that someone would just be there? They wouldn't have to say a word, just stay by your side. That would be enough.

I thought of that while reading the story of Jesus in the Garden of Gethsemane. It's one of the saddest stories in the Bible, and one of the most real.

It tells of the night before Jesus was arrested. He knows what's coming. The political tide has turned against him. The religious establishment considers him a menace; they want him eliminated. He is sure one of his 12 best disciples is about to betray him.

I sense that this was as dark a time as any for Jesus, perhaps as depressing as being on the cross, because this was when his friends turned their backs on him.

We all know the feeling.

Jesus had climbed up the Mount of Olives and taken along his best friends: Peter, James and John. These guys had been with him for three years. They had watched him heal the sick, bring the dead back to life, and stir the hearts of thousands as he preached and practiced the kind of love the world had never seen.

They were convinced that he was the son of God.

Now, Jesus had a simple request.

"Sit here while I pray," he said, according to the Gospel of Mark.

Is that too much to ask?

I don't think so.

But as I read the accounts in three different Gospels, I thought of times when people asked me to just listen, to just take time for them, to treat them as if they mattered.

I remember some of the nights near the end of my father's life, when his body was ravaged by stroke, heart failure and circulation problems. I remember him wanting me to just sit by his bed, and I made excuses to leave the room.

Or, I'd stick my head in, see how he was doing, maybe hold his hand for a few minutes, then head back to my room and try to get some sleep.

He was scared; I was tired.

A football coach once said, "Fatigue makes cowards of us all."

Amen to that.

That's how it was for Jesus that night.

"Sit here while I pray," he told them. "My soul is overwhelmed with sorrow to the point of death."

Jesus was their leader. They had never seen him so exhausted, so needy.

What was their response?

They fell asleep.

He had just been praying that God the Father "have this cup pass from my lips."

Christians believe Jesus knew he had to die to atone for the sins of humanity. Historians agree that Jesus clearly could see the end was near.

His friends were oblivious.

Three times, he asked them to keep their eyes open, to bring their hearts in line with his. Three times he left them, came back, and found they were napping. Three times he reached out to them, and not once did any of them say, "Hey, I'll pray with you. I'll sit right next to you."

He just wanted them near; they just wanted to go to bed.

"Simon," he called to his friend, Peter. "Can you not keep watch for one hour? Watch and pray so that you won't fall into temptation. The spirit is willing, the body is weak."

Sometimes, I think those are some of the truest words ever spoken: The spirit is willing, the body is weak.

And sometimes, my spirit leaves a lot to be desired, too.

Like when my wife wants to talk, and I decide it's far more important to read the paper or make yet another phone call. Or when someone just wants to tell me his troubles, not really expecting me to fix them, but my reaction is, "Hey, what do you want me to do about it?"

The more I read the story of Jesus in the Garden, the more I identify with the sleeping disciples.

I also find it reassuring that Jesus asks his father to get him out of a tight jam, even though he knows he has to endure the ordeal.

And I wish I could say, as Jesus did, "Father, for you, everything is possible. . . . Yet not what I want, but thy will be done."

He says this prayer at least twice, knowing it will not be granted.

The Gospel of Luke reports that Jesus was "sweating blood" during this time of prayer. Some believe that's actual blood; others say it's a phrase from that time when the sweat would just ooze out of your skin and pour off you in huge drops.

Whatever the case, clearly Jesus was in utter psychological agony. He was pacing. His heart was probably racing. He was fearing his prayers would not be answered.

And he was feeling abandoned.

The scene in the garden ends with a bunch of soldiers show-

ing up, led by Judas, who was one of Jesus' 12 disciples. He had
sold Jesus out for 30 pieces of silver, telling the armed guards to
arrest the man he kisses.

Judas betrayed Jesus with a kiss. Peter, James and John did
it with a complete disregard for his feelings. Later, they would
deny him in other ways.

Yet, Jesus remained patient with them. He forgave them
when they asked for forgiveness. He turned Peter and John into
great leaders of the church.

That gives hope to all of us, even when we feel as if we're
sleeping through our own lives.

Saturday, March 16, 2002

PRAYER

God is Not an ATM

It's a little book about a little prayer—the kind that seems perfect for the back pocket of your jeans.

The Prayer of Jabez.

In the Bible, you find the prayer buried in a numbing list of names in the Old Testament, 1 Chronicles 4:10.

Lately, you can see the prayer on top of the best-seller lists of the *New York Times*, *USA Today* and *Publisher's Weekly*.

Sheer numbers? More than 4 million copies sold of a small book about an obscure prayer.

Author Bruce Wilkinson would say all this just proves God's hand is on it—the book, the sales, the impact.

Jabez asked God: "Oh, that You would bless me indeed and enlarge my territory, that Your hand be with me, and that You would keep me from evil, that I may not cause pain."

That's the prayer, start to finish.

Thousands of people say it has changed their lives.

On the Web site www.prayerofjabez.com there are countless testimonials. I began to print them out, and stopped when I noticed there were 41 pages' worth, single-spaced:

- False witness confesses after five years; imprisoned man released
- Job applicant's prayer is heard

• College tuition paid by wealthy benefactor
• God protects driver who falls asleep

That gives you the flavor of what people say has happened after they began to say the prayer for 30 days, which is what the author suggests.

I first heard about the prayer nearly two years ago. A middle-aged friend was struggling with his job. He longed for God "to expand my territory." He really prayed for a job in ministry, or something of service to others, and he prayed like Jabez.

About six months later, he was hired by a ministry, his first job in the field.

This seems like a classic Jabez story, a man with the heart of God longing to serve God. And there seems little doubt that God loves to answer those prayers.

But there is something else happening with this book, this prayer. There is a doctrine that is basically, "Name it, claim it."

That makes me nervous. I sense some of the attraction of Jabez is: Lord, bless me with a new (job, car, house, etc.).

"Is the message that we should pray for a BMW? No, but if that's what you want, ask for it, and if that would convince you of God's love, then it might be granted," David Kopp, the co-author of the book, told the *Fort Worth Star-Telegram*.

I hope Kopp didn't quite mean that the way it sounded, because it sure sounds as if we're supposed to be asking God to prove Himself to us.

If you believe God is in charge, He doesn't have to prove anything to anyone.

Jabez's prayer is more like a request for God to give us a chance to work for Him, and that He keep us safe and from causing pain while doing it.

The Jabez stories that seem most meaningful come from those who prayed like Jabez, and then found chances to express their faith in some of the most unusual circumstances—either to total strangers or to people who have been resisting spiritual discussions for years.

But suppose you pray for something, and God doesn't grant the wish.

Does that mean there's something wrong with you? If God really loved you, then your bid on that lakefront lot would have been accepted, right?

You can see the problems.

Anyone who has ever suffered any sort of serious setback knows that God is not an ATM machine. To know God, we have to figure out who He is and how He operates—instead of trying to make Him into what we want Him to be.

When the authors published the book, they didn't dream of a best-seller list. They prayed that the book would reach people with the message about God, and that it would drive them to prayer. The first printing was 30,000 copies.

It does seem that only divine intervention could have turned this book into mega-seller, with no end in sight.

What makes the book popular is that many want to believe that God cares about them, that God will put a hand on their lives and lead them.

But, sometimes, we don't want to go where He's pointing us.

Jesus didn't say, "Hop in my Lexus and ride with me."

Some of those using the Jabez prayer need to remember that.

Saturday, June 2, 2001

We often hear about God's love for us . . .

How we matter to God . . .

How God has blessed us, sometimes outrageously.

All of this is true, and countless sermons have been preached about it.

But what about when God says no?

What about the nights when we lie in bed, staring at the ceiling, wondering if God is there? Is God listening? Does God care?

Or the times in the hospital when the baby is dying, when the young mother of four probably won't survive, when all the prayers for healing have come back stamped "Rejected"?

These questions are on the minds of many believers. Most are afraid to bring them up because it implies a lack of faith. But people do want to talk about these things, even if there are no good answers.

In church or temple, we often are afraid to bring up such subjects. The Rev. Joey Johnson, pastor of The House of the Lord in Akron, once preached about how "we just talk, mask to mask."

With nice clothes and a smiling face, we hide our pain, our doubts and our disappointment with God. But this code of silence is more destructive than an open expression that some may see as a lack of faith.

If you read the Bible, God says no all the time.

He told Moses that he'd never see the Promised Land, even though Moses clearly was one of God's favorites and sacrificed so much for Him. I always thought Moses got a bad break, especially compared with some biblical figures such as the lying, scheming Jacob, who was able to die in comfort with his family around him.

After King David had an affair that produced a child, he prayed for a week for the life of the ill infant. The baby died. Many read that and say, "Why kill the baby when the parents were the sinners?"

Paul prayed three times for the removal of "a thorn in the flesh." Scholars have killed millions of trees writing papers as they guess about "the thorn," which is never identified in the New Testament. But the real point isn't the thorn. It's that God didn't answer Paul's prayer—other than to say, "My grace is sufficient."

Many times, that is true.

But when you're in the midst of a crisis, you really don't want to hear it. You don't believe it. You just wonder why someone won't take the hurt away.

During the 4½ years after my father's stroke, I prayed for healing.

I prayed for him to just sleep through the night without waking up in a frightening fit of coughing where it seemed he was about to gag up a lung. I prayed for God to let him die. I prayed for relief, for him and me.

I usually heard nothing.

Now, I can see that if my father had died or been healed even three years into the ordeal, I never would have come to a real faith. Nor would my father. It was only through feeling helpless that we became serious with God, and that happened in the last six months of his life.

I went to God in desperation because there was nowhere else to turn. I began to study the Bible, to talk to some real men of faith (not perfect, just genuine), and this experience changed the spiritual life of my father, my wife and myself.

A pastor named Rick Warren once wrote, "God is more concerned with your character than your comfort or your success."

Changing diapers, cleaning beds, cutting up food and helping my father in so many other ways taught me much about humility, suffering and how to serve others. And it taught me to appreciate people like caretakers who have endured these trials seemingly forever. I didn't feel very successful or comfortable, but the experience did improve my character.

When I speak to inmates as part of my prison ministry, I often ask, "Do you learn more from good times or bad times?"

To a man, the answer is hard times.

So many people in biblical times—and probably now—only connect with God when they feel the walls closing in and can't find anyone who understands.

We sometimes can see that God's no was the right answer, though it took years for us to figure that out.

But not always.

Some things just seem senseless. Sometimes, we pray for patience and grace, and just experience more pressure and heartache. Some days, maybe even some years, nothing adds up.

Our prayers aren't selfish; our motives are pure. But God still says no.

Someone dies. Someone is laid off and a better job doesn't come. Someone watches a parent drift into the no-man's land of Alzheimer's. Someone close betrays us. Or maybe we hurt people and want to reconcile, but they won't even hear our apology.

I have no quick answers for this, and mistrust anyone who does.

About the only thing I know is, life is a mess—period.

But if you believe in heaven, then you can try to take some comfort in knowing that what's happening today is not the last chapter of your story.

We can either go through it with God or by ourselves.

It was no vague metaphor when Jesus talked about carrying a cross. God does help us cope by sending his people to just be there—not to fix us or spout off a Bible verse and then walk away. Even Simon came along to take the load off Jesus, if just for a little while. That is how some of my friends have helped me.

But there are times when I feel like the apostles who had just heard a tough sermon from Jesus, which caused the crowd to walk away—grumbling.

In the book of John, Chapter 6, Jesus turned to his core group and asked, "Are you going to leave, too?"

Peter answered, "Lord, where else can we go?"

That question still matters today.

Saturday, January 25, 2003

Clergy: Your People Want to Know What Happens to Their Prayers

I'm addressing this story to priests, pastors, rabbis, imams, etc.

Your people want to hear about prayers that don't seem to be answered. They want to know that they are not alone, that others also have had that feeling of dropping off God's radar screen. They're not so much angry as they are seeking hope.

They want to know they still matter to God, and the trials they are facing will end and there is a purpose behind it.

That's what I learned from my previous column, called, "When God says no."

More than 40 calls and e-mails came in.

One local minister took me to task for writing "God says no all the time in the Bible."

OK, it's not all the time. I just went over the top on that.

God answers far more prayers than we remember. Pastor Ron Fowler of Arlington Church of God recently preached: "We sometimes act like teen-agers. All week, you can tell a teen-ager yes, but, come the weekend, we say no just once, and they scream as if we never give them anything."

So true.

But most of those who responded to the column are like the man who went through four funerals in four months—cancer being the main culprit.

"Early, I prayed for their health and recovery," the person wrote. "As it was clear those prayers went in the Reject Pile, I began to pray that they wouldn't hurt so much. Then I figured out that God's will—and, in some cases, our family's stubborn streak—was guiding their lives to the very end.

"I started praying like a kid wanting a pony for Christmas, and ended up saying thank you for a pair of socks and a warm coat."

As he watched many of these people come to peace with their own deaths, he realized: "My prayers were answered."

Another man wrote about reading the Prayer of Jabez every day. It asks God to bless us and enlarge our territory.

"Then I lost my job of 22 years that was paying $200,000," he wrote. "Last year, I made $16,000. That sounded like a 'No' to me, but it's not the end of the story."

He said his old job was wearing him out, taking him on the road too often and taking him away from his family. He is now opening his own business.

"No money yet," he wrote. "But I am home every night and, like Abraham did in faithful obedience, I am striking out into a foreign land and counting on God's providence."

The stories just kept coming.

A mother recently lost her son in a car crash: "I did all the things the Bible, the preacher and the other people in church said to keep him safe . . . praying at the altar, direct line to God. . . . I'm told not to question, just to believe, and that's very hard to do."

It should be mentioned that just because we wonder what God is doing or why something happened in our lives, it doesn't mean we have lost our faith. I'm sure my wife has questioned some of the things I've done, yet she doesn't doubt the validity of our marriage. In fact, it gets stronger when we talk about it.

I read the mother's letter to the Rev. Knute Larson, pastor of The Chapel in Akron. His mother died when he was 21; his sister died when he was 17.

"I still question God about that, and it was 40-some years ago," Larson said. "Forget the people who tell you not to ask 'why' to God. You may not get an answer, but you can ask. I go to Psalm 73. I don't always get the answers I want, but in the end, I just decide to trust God. The Bible tells us that all of creation groans, and it does at times like this."

Larson then said: "I heard a TV preacher say every Christian should be happy and healthy. Where is that in the Bible?"

Where indeed?

The man who gave me my first full-time newspaper job, in Greensboro, N.C., was Irwin Smallwood. He read my column and wrote about his 53-year marriage. For the last seven years, he's been dealing with his wife's slippage into Alzheimer's. Sometimes she knows him, sometimes not.

"I pray for her deliverance, of course, and pray for her peace until deliverance comes," he wrote. "One day, my preacher daughter said, 'Remember, Dad, you're not in charge anymore.' I thank God that I realized this early on and it has carried me this far."

We hate to admit it, but we are not in charge.

There is so little that is really under our control that it's scary to think about it. One car wreck, one word from the doctor, one telephone call in the dead of night is all we need to remember that.

Another man wrote of spending six years going from doctor to doctor trying to find out what was wrong. Finally, they figured it out: He has multiple sclerosis.

"I heard that and was angry at God, at life, at my faith, at everything," he wrote. "I had been an athlete in my younger days, and now it was difficult to walk down the hallway without falling down. It was so unfair."

Then his faith began to grow, and he saw God working to lead him to one of the top specialists in this field.

"Am I glad I have MS? Of course not," he wrote. "I pray every day for healing. But I'm learning so much, depending upon God to help with simple things, like keeping my balance, both physically and spiritually. I'm learning that His timing is everything."

He added that God has his attention, and "He is giving me strength to help other people with MS not to give up."

Rabbi Arthur Lavinsky of Beth El Congregation in Akron said: "Some people point to the Holocaust as evidence there is no God, but every survivor I know—and I know many—has said their faith helped them through it. Some of the people who wonder where God is during a tragedy didn't consult with God much before it happened."

Life is not fair. We don't know all the answers.

Lavinsky and Larson both said we may not find all the answers in this life, but we must keep talking to God about it—even if we don't always like what we hear back.

Saturday, February 8, 2003

Not Every Prayer Ends in a Miracle, But Sometimes They Help Us Face Another Day

When my father was dying, I wish I had prayed with him more.

Not because it would heal him, at least not his body.

But I know now, prayer was what he really needed.

He needed to connect with God, because he was going to meet God soon.

I needed to connect with God, because I knew he was going to meet God.

Most of us have an urge to connect with God because most of us are convinced we'll eventually face God.

I don't care how long you've been in church or how deep your faith is, there is something scary about that.

And I know prayer helps.

I can't say that it always heals. I can't say why we pray for some people and they die—and why we pray for others and they live.

I can't tell you much about prayer.

Other than it does help.

Newsweek magazine is saying much the same thing in its current cover story: "God & Health: Is Religion Good Medicine? Why Science Is Starting to Believe."

As you'd expect, the story is long on debate. There are opinions from several medical people, along with some doctors who don't see any benefit, but it is worth reading.

The most concrete research reveals those who attend a worship service one to two times a week live longer than those who don't, especially those who have given up on faith.

Some explain it by saying people who are serious about their faith tend to live healthier lifestyles, at least in terms of staying away from smoking, drinking and drugs.

When it comes to healing, the research is not as strong.

But prayer never hurts unless you attach some sort of twisted guilt trip to it, such as, "Your baby is sick because God is punishing you for sin in your own life."

How would that person know? In the Old Testament, Job heard that from his "friends" and it was as wrong then as it often is today.

Most medical people see something good about prayer as it relates to healing, recovery, life span and a general sense of peace.

Even if they can't say what.

But this is a very personal issue.

Someone you love is facing major surgery. Or you feel your health slipping away. You are scared.

What do you do?

Like most of us, you find the best medical treatment.

And you pray.

If you haven't been in that situation, just wait.

You will.

You may have long given up on God or decided it's all just a myth. But then you hear the word "cancer," and there will be something tugging at your heart, something that will make you want to talk to God—even if you can't find the words.

I love the passage from the Bible's book of Romans 8:26, which reads: "The Spirit helps us in our weakness. We don't know what we ought to pray for, but the Spirit intercedes for us with groans that words cannot express."

That means those times when we say, "Oh, God . . ."

All we can do is moan, but those sounds become very powerful prayers. They're often more meaningful than all the flowery, structured prayers said in some churches and healing services.

They're prayers from the deepest parts of our soul, prayers of agony and despair, prayers that mean so much even if we seem to say so little in terms of actual words.

Often, those prayers aren't answered as we hoped.

The baby dies. The cancer spreads. The job is lost. The child doesn't kick drugs.

But those prayers do heal us because they do something very important—they help us to face the next day.

Saturday, November 8, 2003

If You Want the Kids to Pray, You'd Better Pray with Them at Home

As I watched the demonstrations over removal of a Ten Commandments monument from an Alabama government building, I thought: How many of those people have the Ten Commandments posted in their own homes?

This is not to debate the legal issues; it's just a question.

If the Ten Commandments are important—and many of us would agree with that—how many of us have them on our own walls?

I don't.

How many of us can name all 10?

I was able to do it quickly before I wrote this column, but that's because I recently had to look them up for another reason.

A couple of years ago, however, someone challenged me to list all 10.

It took 10 to 15 minutes, and I was stuck at nine.

I wish the reason I couldn't recall the one about coveting was because I'm just a content guy, never jealous. But I don't want to break the commandment about bearing false witness, which is the Ninth Commandment—at least, I think it's No. 9.

Please, don't ask me to list the commandments in order.

Maybe you can do it. Maybe you had the order drilled into you as a child, so you'll never forget. Maybe you are a person who remembers things like that.

But go ahead, try to name all 10, right now. It's not as easy as many of us believe.

Regardless of where we stand on the Ten Commandments being in courthouses, no one stops us from displaying them in our homes, or even discussing them with our kids.

But not many of us do so.

It's much like the issue of prayer in schools.

How many of us who gnash our teeth about the lack of prayer in school actually pray with our family?

And I don't mean prayers like, "Bless us, our Lord, and these thy gifts, pass the meat and potatoes real quick."

I mean when the family gets together and spends a few moments talking to God, perhaps with everyone praying about what is in his or her heart.

Some people who want prayer in schools don't believe in praying out loud at home. If that's the case, why ask the schools to do it for you?

I'm just speaking from personal experience: My wife, Roberta, and I began praying together and out loud several years ago and it has helped cement our marriage.

Other couples have told me the same story: how a prayer at the start of day . . . how two people holding hands, closing eyes and just talking to God, often praying for each other . . . how this creates a sense of peace and compassion for each other.

In the beginning, it feels very strange and makes most people self-conscious. But God's spirit eventually takes over for those who stick with it.

What's the point of all this?

It's that we really control our own spiritual lives.

The Ten Commandments hanging on the wall may be important symbolically, but the way to keep our kids out of that courtroom is to talk about the Ten Commandments at home and to live them out as best we can.

We may attach great significance to prayer in school. And I

think a moment of silence at the start of each day—or even each class—is an idea worth pursuing.

But if we want kids to pray, then we better pray with the kids at home—and do it sincerely.

Men are especially timid in the area of prayer. Somehow, that's fallen into the category of something women do, and we just sort of stand off to the side, or just go watch a ball game.

But in terms of how children grow in areas of faith, what the mother and father do (or don't do) with the family spiritually is far more crucial than what happens in the arena of politics.

We can't count on public institutions to educate our children about these issues because court rulings and waves of opinion change.

Our faith, if real, should not.

Saturday, September 6, 2003

How We Approach God Can Show Us What Kind of Faith We Have

Did you ever notice that those who seem to have the least pray the most?

Their faith runs deep. Their prayers are sincere, trusting, confident.

And often, their life is a mess.

No money, declining health, old age.

But they pray, not so much for God to change things, but just for God to be there, for God to help them endure their pain.

Me?

I pray for God to fix this, take care of that.

I come to Him as if He were the Great Dentist in the sky. I open my mouth and say, "God, see this cavity? Fill it up, but whatever You do, don't hurt me."

Then, I wonder if He's listening. I ask why He dared to upset my life by allowing whatever inconvenience happens to be annoying me.

And when He doesn't work on my timetable, I stare at the heavens and think, "Hey, *are you on vacation*, or what? Anybody up there working at all?"

And then, there are moments of doubt.

Is *anybody* up there?

I'm like a character in the New Testament parable in which a man brings his demon-possessed son to Jesus.

"Can I heal him?" asks the incredulous Jesus. "Ye of little faith."

"I do believe," says the man, "but help me with unbelief."

That's my prayer this Thanksgiving weekend. It's for more

faith, more trust, more of a sense of all the times when God has been there for me—instead of keeping a list when the Almighty decided to leave me alone.

It is a strange thing, trying to have a relationship with God.

My favorite Christian author, Philip Yancey, writes about it in his *Reaching for an Invisible God*. He discusses the elderly women in his church who flock to prayer meetings. They take turns spending all night talking to God, praising God, begging God, thanking God.

No doubt, these women have seen many prayers answered.

But a lot of their prayers seemingly have been ignored. There were children who never did get off drugs, husbands who kept drinking, marriages that shattered, hearts that broke, illnesses that ended in death.

Yet, they pray.

They seem to think that prayer might not be all they want, but it's enough.

I pray, but I don't feel I'm very good at it. Sometimes, I feel as if my prayers just sound stupid to God. Or I feel as if I have no right to ask an Almighty God to take a couple of minutes from the business of running the universe to hear about my problem on the job.

And, sometimes, I pray and feel nothing at all.

Someone recently told me, "I have a hard time with all this God stuff because I can't see it."

He recently had tried to commit suicide. He was beyond despair, heading into spiritual numbness, but still he wanted me to pray with him—mostly because he didn't know what else to do.

So we prayed, and, frankly, I'm not sure what God made of it.

I thought about that on Monday, flying home from covering the Browns game in Baltimore.

I don't have a clue about why a jet stays up in the air. Or how a pilot can know from 30,000 feet where the jet is supposed to land, when houses look like matchboxes and cars look like ants, when no people are in sight.

None of that makes sense to me.

But the pilot brought the jet down early in the morning in fog that was so thick, I was staring out the window yet never saw the ground until the *clank* of the wheels on the runway.

They say it's radar, but it seemed like a miracle to me.

On the other hand, I also saw the sun rise above the clouds and didn't think twice about it.

As I write this, I wonder what God thinks about me being more impressed with radar and the pilot than with His bringing up the sun each day.

I know this is Thanksgiving weekend, and I'm thankful to have landed on Monday. I'm thankful to have been on a jet that morning of September 11 and not on one of the four that crashed. I even ended up at my destination.

I don't spend much time thinking about why my jet didn't crash when others did. I have no answer. Maybe there are no answers.

Instead, I tell myself to be thankful to God for all the blessings in my life. For my wife. My job. My house. My health.

But on and on it goes, *my* this, *my* that.

Part of me seems to say to God, "Hey, I'll give you all the thanks, just don't disturb me and *my* way of doing things."

I often pray to put things in God's hands, then I take them back. I tell God that I want to be a better person, but sometimes I do it like this: "God, please give me patience, and do it *right now*!"

I've found that my best prayers tend to be the most honest ones, even the ones that I have absolutely zero faith that God will answer—such as with that guy who found he "couldn't even kill (himself) right."

At times like that, I find myself being like those old women in church, thanking God for just being God, even when it seems He's not paying much attention to us right now.

And I suppose that's how He wants us to be.

Saturday, November 24, 2001

Pick Those Numbers and Say Your Prayers: Some Find God When The Lottery's Involved

A recent lottery winner said, "God and I are on good terms today."

Bet God was relieved to hear that.

It's hard to know exactly what God thinks of lottery winners, but odds are, He's not thrilled with having His name tossed into the middle of Buckeye 5, Pick 3, Pick 4, Super Lotto Plus and whatever other rackets are being used to lure people to throw their money away.

"The first thing I did was thank God," said Dave Edwards, a Kentucky resident who won $73 million in the Powerball drawing last month.

Edwards added, "I was down to my last three unemployment checks. I was out of medical insurance. My back was against the wall."

So he spent $8 on Powerball tickets and prayed for a winner: "Help me, Lord. I know this might not be right for me to ask You, but can You just let me win this?"

Not exactly as eloquent as the 23rd Psalm, is it?

But did God answer that prayer?

If so, why Edwards? Why not someone else, whose circumstances were just as desperate, or maybe even worse?

Edwards served 10 years for bank robbery and had other prison stints. He also had a conviction for being a felon and carrying a firearm.

He's not exactly the wife of a firefighter who died in the line of duty, a widow who's now trying to raise three kids by herself. No doubt, someone like that played the lottery.

Or how about this?

If we pray, buy our tickets, and lose—then what? Does that mean God doesn't love us?

There is an area church that holds a drawing during the service, with "lucky" people in the pews winning cash prizes. Don't you think that just about everyone in that church sends up a quick prayer as the winner is about to be named?

And what about the losers?

Does God have something against them?

If God wanted to control and endorse the lottery, why would He pick someone like Mack Metcalf, another Kentucky man, who won $65 million last year.

Metcalf has been charged with failure to pay $31,000 in child support and driving under the influence. He has sued a woman to whom he supposedly gave $500,000 while having a few adult beverages to celebrate his new wealth.

Sure, a guy like that can use the cash, but how will he use it?

The powers behind the lottery love it when someone like Edwards or Metcalf wins. They tend to prey upon people who are down to their last prayer, people who are so desperate that they call out—not to God—but to the higher power of the Wheel of Fortune to save them.

Look at some of the people who line up at most convenience stores to buy lottery tickets, those who are there every week. Too often they are the ones who can least afford the tickets, the ones whose Social Security checks or paychecks are already stretched thin. When some of these people win, they don't even take the cash—they just buy more tickets.

In the recent $300 million Powerball lottery, there were only four winners out of 75 million who purchased tickets.

That's right, four out of 75 million.

"Given what has happened to some of the lottery winners," said Pastor Bud Olszewski of Rittman's Grace Brethren Church, "maybe God answers their prayers by them not winning because He saves them from ruin."

Maybe so.

But when God watches the lottery, He probably shakes his head and says, "This is a con job, and just leave Me out of it."

That's good advice—for all of us.

Saturday, September 8, 2001

Maybe you have always had a close relationship with God. You've always known how to pray, and never doubt that He listens.

You don't have to read the rest of this story.

As for the rest of us . . .

Those of us who sometimes find it very strange to sit in a room alone and try to talk to someone we're not even sure is there . . .

Those of us who would rather have our front teeth knocked out with a jackhammer than pray aloud . . .

Those who us who don't understand the idea of prayer . . .

There's hope.

So say several religious leaders, starting with the Rev. Ronald Fowler from the Arlington Church of God.

"You have to start with prayer being communication with God," Fowler says.

But how do you communicate with someone you don't see?

"That's a good question," he says. "It goes to your idea of God. Too many people see God as this harsh judge, and they're afraid they'll say something wrong. Or they think you have to pray these long, formalized prayers. They find the whole thing intimidating."

So they do nothing.

Until something happens that they can't control.

Something such as waiting for a biopsy to come back or for a wayward adult child to kick drugs. There are few atheists in foxholes or emergency rooms.

"I remember a friend of mine telling me that he didn't want

to die, that he didn't think it was fair, that he still had so much to do," Fowler says. "But he had a terminal disease. I told him that I didn't want to die, either."

The key to prayer is honesty.

"We prayed, but my friend died," Fowler says. "But what I saw was how prayer changed his attitude. He became more accepting, focusing more on the life to come in heaven than the life he was leaving behind. Most often, prayer changes our attitude about our circumstances."

That's not what some people want to hear.

Too many of us have been told that prayer is like an ATM. We hit a few buttons, and out comes the cash to cover all our sins. Name it and claim it, some TV evangelists say.

But often, the ATM is out of order. Or the few pennies we receive back don't come close to buying us out of trouble. And then, we decide prayer just isn't worth the time.

Don't give up.

That's the word from the Rev. Gordon Yahner of St. Hilary Catholic Church in Fairlawn.

"I'm not the last word in prayer, and a lot of people think they are," he says. "But when you don't know what to do, show up (for prayer) and let God do the rest."

"You can do it with your eyes open, or closed," says Dr. Jay Groat of Akron's First Congregational Church. "Closed-eye prayer is more formal, in church or when you kneel at your bed. But open-eyed prayer is the conversations we have with ourselves in our head as we go through the day."

Have those conversations with God. That's what the Apostle Paul meant when he wrote, "Pray unceasingly."

No one judges the silent prayers. And if you believe most religions, God is glad to hear our prayers—any prayers.

"But most of us have to admit we don't make the time to pray," says Pastor Tony Naska of Middlebury Chapel in Akron.

"Our days are filled with our jobs, TV, CDs, video games, the Internet. Being quiet is foreign to us."

To combat that, Yahner says he goes to prayer by repeating a Bible verse over and over, as sort of a mantra to clear his head and turn his heart to God.

In the Old Testament's Psalm 46, King David wrote, "Be still and know I am God."

But who wants to do that?

As Naska says: "When we just stop and face ourselves, we see ourselves as God sees us. And we have to confront our fears."

And our sense of failure.

We don't need to be so hard on ourselves—God gets it.

"He just wants us to keep it simple and keep it sincere," Fowler says. "You can even keep it short. But what we all need to do is keep at it."

Saturday, January 20, 2001

I'll pray for you.

How many times have you heard someone say that? How many times have you said it? And how many times have you actually prayed for the person?

I don't want the IRS auditing my account on this item.

Most of the time, when someone says they'll pray for me, I want to believe it. But I sort of doubt it.

Countless times, people have asked me to pray for them . . .

And I said I would . . .

And I didn't.

The words sometimes sound lame as they come from my lips: "I'll pray for you."

I've even said it to people to shut them up. They start telling me their troubles. I've heard some of the problems before. Or, maybe, I just don't want to hear them now.

And I know I can't do anything about them.

"That's too bad," I say. "I'll pray for you."

And I'm gone.

Great. "I'll pray for you" has been turned into an exit line. I bet God is thrilled with that.

I've had people tell me, "I'm praying for you." And I'm amazed they'd take time to pray for me, given all the problems they must have in their own lives.

These people usually are very dedicated to their prayer life. They keep lists. They look at the names and the notes next to the names. They take time to raise those names and prayers to God.

I'm not one of those people.

I doubt most people are those people.

So what does it mean to say, "I'll pray for you"?

Absolutely nothing—unless someone actually prays. Pray right on spot A few years ago, I heard a minister admit he had a lousy memory and rarely remembered to pray for anyone. That did wake up the folks in the pews, a few of whom were probably praying for a shorter sermon.

The minister said his new approach was this: If someone asks him to pray, he prays.

Right then.

He may take the person's hands and just pray for him. Or put a hand on the person's shoulder. He'll make some sort of contact and then raise words and hearts to the Lord.

Why not?

How long does it take? You don't have to recite the entire Old Testament. Just pray: Someone is sick, someone just lost a job, someone is thankful.

Take a moment, talk to God about it.

At the very least, you kept your word. You promised to pray, and you did. And the person knows you prayed because the person was there with you—hopefully, praying, too.

Several years ago, I was going through a spiritual crisis as my father was in a long battle with a stroke that eventually led to his death. I mentioned the trials and frustrations to a member of the clergy, who sympathized and promised to pray for me.

And he was gone.

I told this story to a friend, who at the time was challenging me to read the Bible, to get serious about faith.

"You mean the guy didn't even pray with you?" he asked.

I shrugged.

"Let's pray now," he said.

He took my hands. He prayed that I'd have the strength to

handle whatever came next, that God would help me financially with the mounting bills, and that my father would find peace and comfort as he dealt with the debilitating stroke.

I'm sure he stumbled around through the prayer, but it sounded like poetry. This guy was talking to God for me.

"That's prayer," he said. "Talking to God with respect, but also like you know God."

For years, I was uncomfortable praying out loud. I figured I sounded stupid to the people around me, but even dumber to God.

I finally came to the conclusion that God isn't grading on style points.

It's the heart.

Now, I try to pray for people on the spot. A few months ago, a woman at a fast food place told me about raising a child alone and how she had applied for a new job with more pay. She asked me to pray for her.

Right at the drive-through window, I prayed something about getting the job, taking care of her daughter and giving her peace about what happened. It took about 30 seconds.

A week later, she said, "Hey, I got that job. Thanks for the prayer."

I felt better than she did—at least at that moment.

Some people can pray up a storm; others do it in barely a whisper.

Don't compare yourself to others. Besides, God seems to favor the person in the back of the church, head down, heart breaking, the only words coming out being: "Lord, I am a sinner; God, please help me . . ."

Yes, God does hear our prayers, even if he doesn't answer them as we want, or when we want.

I need to keep reminding myself of that because it's so easy not to pray, or just to run through some ragged prayer like: "Bless us, Lord, and these thy gifts, pass the corn, and don't forget the fish."

There have been times when I've tried to pray about something and didn't know what to say. The situation was such a hopeless mess, words seemed useless. Often, praying with someone else, letting them pray for me, has helped me.

Having guts enough to ask someone to pray along with you—that may be one of the best prayers of all.

Saturday, October 26, 2002

When You've Prayed Enough to Pave the Road to Heaven, Pray On

Are you praying for somebody?

A child who no longer is so young anymore, but still acts like it?

A father who walked out of your life years ago, and never came back?

A brother who can't stay out of jail? A sister who can't stay sober? A friend who keeps going broke?

Isn't there always somebody?

You want to help these people. You may have invested too much in some of them: Too much time, too much money, and most of all—too much of your heart.

In some ways, you may be relieved they are out of your life for now.

But there are nights when you can't sleep, when you try to read but the words don't register. So you stare at the ceiling.

And you begin to pray for them.

You may have run out of words. Your faith meter may be on empty. But suddenly, you just have to cry out, "God, please help them!"

You sometimes weep more than pray.

Help him to be a father to his kids, not to skip the weekend visit like he's done so many times before.

Help her to not play games with the kids, to realize that I have divorced her, but I didn't divorce them.

Help her to be serious about the rehabilitation program.

Help him to hold his temper and keep his job.

Help my son to know that I still love him.

Help my daughter to know that she can come home, the door is open.

When former Tribe pitcher Herb Score was struck in the eye with a baseball hit by another player, he cried out to Jude—the patron saint of lost causes, according to Roman Catholic tradition.

Don't we all know someone who seems like a lost cause, yet they still have a grip on our hearts?

These people may have hurt us. They certainly have let some of us down. They seem to be wasting their lives. Part of us says we shouldn't care about them anymore.

But we can't quite let go.

So we pray.

So, if prayer is so great, then why have you been praying for that son of yours for 20 years and he's still doing crack and running the streets?

If prayer works, then why is your daughter so lost, so depressed, so disconnected from the people who really do love her? Why does she give herself to men who just abuse her?

If there is a God, why doesn't he just fix it?

Part of the problem is God listens to our prayers, but those we pray for don't hear the voice of God. Just as they may have tuned out you and so many others who reached out.

So we weep. If not on the outside, certainly deep in our souls.

We need verses like this from Isaiah, Chapter 25: "The Sovereign Lord will wipe away the tears from all the faces."

Or this from Revelation, Chapter 21: God "will wipe every tear from their eyes. There will be no more death or mourning or crying for pain, for the old order of things has passed away."

There are stories of people who are living, breathing, vibrant testimonies to prayer. But others are still wandering in a spiritual desert.

So don't discourage the mother who has been praying for that child for decades. Don't tell that person how you'd feel if you were in her place, because you're not.

Just stand with them, pray with them, hug them. That's what they need most from us.

Saturday, November 22, 2003

HOLIDAYS

Mary and Joseph Weren't Perfect, but God Still Chose Them

My family's not Ozzie and Harriet.

How many times have you heard that? Or maybe even said that?

I recently was reading Luke's account of the Christmas story, and those words came back to me.

This sure wasn't Ozzie and Harriet.

Mary was a teen-ager—most historians believe she was between 14 and 16. Joseph was a few years older. Based on the culture of 2,000 years ago, the marriage was probably arranged, with Mary's parents paying Joseph's parents as part of the wedding deal.

I have a friend who is a priest and a native of India, where he serves God today. When he made the decision to be a priest, his father became very upset.

Why?

Because it would cost the family money!

My friend is college-educated, and he was a very attractive free agent for wealthy families who wanted to make an excellent match for their daughters. The father was considering several lucrative offers to marry off his son when the son decided to follow God's call to the priesthood and a ministry of taking care of poor widows and their children.

His family was proud of his heart, but this was an economic

setback for them. For several years, there was strain between the father and son.

This happened only 20 years ago.

That wasn't exactly Ozzie and Harriet, either.

Back to Mary and Joseph.

Their marriage was set, the deal was cut, and everyone was supposed to live happily ever after.

Only God dropped into Mary's life in the form of an angel, telling her that he wanted her to give birth to a son who would be the Messiah, even though, in her words, "I have not known a man."

Mary was scared and confused. Buying into this plan would kill her marriage to Joseph, damage her social standing in her village and probably ruin her life.

In one of the greatest statements of faith, Mary risked her future and was willing to suffer disgrace to follow God. Most people in her village would have considered her immoral or crazy, or both.

Joseph found out his fiancee was pregnant and knew there was no need for a DNA test. In that culture, he couldn't even touch his fiancee before the wedding because the women of the village made it a mission to keep an eye on the couple and keep them a safe distance apart.

Joseph was ready to dump Mary quietly and check the rest of the field. No doubt, his family supported that idea. If nothing else, going back on the open marriage market would probably mean more money for his family, and certainly less shame and heartache.

But God spoke to Joseph through an angel. Joseph agreed to go on with the wedding despite this messy, embarrassing situation. He knew he would be ridiculed for sticking with his marriage plans, but he did that anyway.

Joseph made one of the gutsiest decisions in biblical history.

*

From reading the Bible, I love how God picks some of the most unlikely people to do his work. These "little people" end up being very big in his plans. Shepherds such as David become kings. Old men such as Moses are drafted into leadership. A humble woman named Esther confronts a king and destroys a plot to kill the Jews.

The first disciples of Jesus were mostly blue-collar guys with more muscles than brains, guys who loved to argue, whose egos often ran amok and who didn't always trust each other. In sports, most of God's selection of people for his key missions would have been initially written off as "a bad draft."

God wants his son to be born in a barn to an unwed teen-aged mother and a modest carpenter?

He wants stuttering Moses to lead the Jews out of slavery? Moses had a murder buried in his background!

He wants whiny Jonah to deliver a message to save a city?

David had a woman problem. Abraham had a truth problem. Jonah had an obedience problem.

One of Jesus' favorite people was Martha, a woman with a busyness problem. She always had to be doing something, even when it was time just to sit back, pray and listen.

As for the 12 apostles, they seem to have had enough problems to keep a battery of psychologists busy for a decade.

Christians talk about the birth of Jesus as the start of the forgiveness of sins and the way to a new life, but the Christmas story is even more than that.

It's God reaching out to very flawed people like us, with something for us to do that is beyond anything we can ever imagine.

Saturday, December 21, 2002

Holiday Baggage: Bad Memories Resurface This Time of Year

There are people who say, "Every time I hear Silent Night or Jingle Bells, I want to throw up."

There's a woman who sees Christmas coming and thinks of a beer can flung against a wall, a ghost of Christmas past.

In my family, Christmas was a time for my father to grab my hand, take me out to the car and wait for my mother to get ready for church. My mother was one of those people who always was 15 minutes late; my father was perpetually 10 minutes early.

And Christmas was about the only time they went to church together, although they didn't exactly walk through the door holding hands. Cold, stony silence was more like it.

Somewhere, Jesus Christ was supposed to be in the middle of all this, but I never saw it.

The Rev. Marshall Brandon thinks of Christmas and flashes back to his "B.C. period . . . as in before I came to Christ."

Brandon remembers Christmas as a time when the booze flowed, when the voices were raised, the words turned ugly.

"Finally, there was violence," he said. "My parents would hit each other. I was just a little kid, and it was like my world was falling apart. They are the two people who are supposed to keep you safe, and they were trying to beat each other. I kept thinking that my parents didn't act like the people on TV, and I wanted that kind of peaceful family."

Now a pastor at Hudson Community Chapel, Brandon said it took "at least five years" for him to leave the baggage of those Christmases behind.

For some people, Christmas is a time of tears.

"I'm very conscious of people losing ones they love to death during this season," said Pastor Knute Larson of The Chapel.

"When I was 24, my mother was dying of cancer," he said. "She was down to about 70 pounds, and she was in bed in the living room, not able to do much of anything."

Death. Drinking. Fighting.

And peace on Earth?

"That's exactly what I wanted," Brandon said. "Peace. I heard the song about peace, and I wanted peace at home."

But too often, that doesn't happen at Christmas.

"Even if it's not the extreme cases, when you have gift-giving tied into the holidays, you have problems," said Rabbi David Horowitz of Temple Israel.

For those of the Jewish faith, this is Hanukkah. It's a "relatively minor holiday," Horowitz said, but it has become a big deal because families gather and gifts are exchanged.

And people become envious, worried, angry.

"They don't know if their gift to someone else will be received well," he said. "And they try not to get upset when the gifts they receive fall below expectations."

In the midst of all this is the usual tension of relatives tossed together. It was once said that families are people with whom you are stuck in an elevator—you'd never choose to hang around with some of them.

But you have no choice.

Some people love this season. They see God's hand in it. Their families aren't perfect, but there are far more hugs than shoves, more kisses than people telling each other to kiss off.

For them, it's easy to see the meaning of Hanukkah. Or, they really do understand Christ's coming. Some of those people go to Harvest House at the Haven of Rest and want to invite a woman and her children into their home.

"Those people mean well, but the last thing our people want to do is be with strangers during this season," said the Haven's

Eileen Thomas. "They just have Christmas horror stories. They just want to be somewhere safe."

Don't we all?

"Christmas is supposed to be about The Good News," Larson said.

Meaning?

"Christ's coming," he said. "A new life for everyone from wise men to shepherds, from one end of society to the other. When my mother died, it was a bad news/good news situation. She left us, but she went to heaven, a place of no pain, of eternal peace."

Or as the Haven's Curt Thomas said, "For the men in our resident program, this is the first time in years they've been sober for Christmas."

And for that, they thank God.

"It doesn't have to be negative," Brandon said. "For those of us who believe, a Savior is born. Lives are changed."

Or as Horowitz said, "It's about the holiday, not about you. We need to remember that."

Saturday, December 23, 2000

The Meaning of Easter is Simple: Hope

For most of my life, Easter was never about God.

Easter was about wearing stiff church clothes and squirming on a hard wooden pew as a pastor droned on and on—sometimes complaining about all the people who come to church on Easter and Christmas, but not the rest of the year.

Easter was about colored eggs and chocolate bunnies. It was about trips to the home of my aunt, where the men cleared the table after dinner so they could play cards while the women did the dishes.

Easter was about sneaking off into the bedroom so I could listen to the Tribe game on the radio. I still remember the Indians winning a game on Easter when a long-forgotten player named Ron Lolich hit a home run.

Easter was about seeing some relatives I loved and others I would just as soon send out to sea in a leaky rowboat, smack into the middle of a hurricane.

Easter was about beets. I hated beets. Even the thought of them today still churns my stomach.

Easter was a holiday, like any other. Despite the trip to church, it had about as much spiritual significance as Groundhog Day.

But what is it really about?

Christians will tell you it's about the cross and the empty tomb. About Jesus, the Son of God, dying for our sins, then rising from the dead.

Or as The Chapel's Knute Larson said, "If it's not true, then I quit."

But what is truth?

Actually, the Roman ruler Pontius Pilate asked that question of Jesus. As reported in John, Chapter 18, he almost spat out the words.

He was too hardened, too cynical to think that this Jewish carpenter who claimed to be the Son of the God could have anything to do with him. He seemed to be a very modern guy whose motto was, "Hey, whatever works."

That sounds good until what works for someone else causes big problems for you—like a bogus sales pitch that leads us to buy something under false pretenses. It works for the salesman, but not the customer.

Then again, isn't life just dog-eat-dog, where only the strong survive? Forrest Gump may say that life is like a box of chocolates, but often, it's more a plate of those dreaded beets. Besides, in the long run, we're all dead, right?

"There has to be more to life than death," Larson said. "Life is sometimes terrible and unfair. Is there just today, or eternity? My mother died too young. My teen-aged sister died. If I didn't believe in the message of Easter, there would be no hope for them—or me."

Or as Father Norm Douglas, an Akron Catholic priest, said, "Life is more than evil and suffering. Life is more than death. Somewhere, down deep, a part of all of us is crying out for something more than just this life, a longing for meaning."

Easter should bring up the centuries-old question: Who was Jesus?

Historians generally agree that there was a real Jesus and that he was an exceptional teacher. But Jesus and his disciples said he was more than that. As famed writer C.S. Lewis often said, Jesus either was the Son of God or he was a lunatic. He either was the Messiah or he had a Messiah complex.

You can't have it both ways, argued Lewis.

"I keep hearing people say that Jesus never claimed to be the

Son of God," Larson said. "But he does so in several places in the Bible."

In the four Gospels, it's obvious the Jewish religious establishment and the Roman officials felt threatened by Jesus because so many Jews claimed they saw him heal people and even bring them back from the dead. The poor wanted him to lead a revolution, to throw out the oppressive Roman government.

For much of his three-year public ministry, Jesus challenged religious leaders and conventional thinking. He called some of them frauds and hypocrites. Journalists like to say part of their job is to comfort the afflicted and afflict the comfortable, but Jesus did that first.

That's why the power structure wanted him eliminated. They brought him up on half-baked charges and broke countless Roman and Jewish legal procedures until they finally got a death sentence.

The Bible says this was destined to happen, that Jesus died for our sins, or, as one of the old hymns claims, "There is power in the blood."

What was that supposed to mean?

I had no problem admitting to being a sinner, even if I loved to deny a lot of my sins. But what did Jesus being executed on the cross have to do with any of that? And what was the big deal about the blood?

It didn't become clear until I spent a year reading the Old Testament. It's hundreds of pages of God trying to bring his people close, his people turning away and then offering all kinds of sacrifices to God as a way of making up for their sins.

These sacrifices included everything from the best crops to the prized animals to Abraham nearly stabbing his own son, until God speaks and tells Abraham to use a ram instead.

During the time of Jesus, people understood sacrifices for forgiveness. At some temples, lambs were sold so people could take them to rabbis, who would kill them as sin offerings. Blood flowed like a river, the Bible says.

The idea of God sending his son to die on a cross as an offering for sin would have made perfect sense 2,000 years ago. That's why some refer to Jesus as the Lamb of God.

Christians say Jesus didn't stay dead and buried.

"You need to understand that in most churches, there is a cross, but Jesus isn't on it," said Dr. Jay Groat of Akron's First Congregational Church. "That's because he has risen."

Or as Paul writes in Romans, Chapter 8, Jesus overcame sin and death, and we can do the same by placing our faith in him.

"Easter is about the birth of something new," said Joey Johnson, pastor of Akron's House of the Lord. "It's about lives that are transformed, about a new life. It's about a lot more than just church. People may be suspicious of churches, but there is a real spiritual hunger. At Easter, we need to address that."

At the Haven of Rest Rescue Mission in Akron, they will serve about 250 meals today. They also will have chapel services before each meal, where the goal is to give people more than just food to chew on.

The Rev. Curt Thomas, the mission's director, talks about people who feel they've had a fruitless past and have a hopeless present; he points them to a future that has direction and meaning.

"We've seen it happen to our men and women for years," he said. "Jesus changes lives."

For that to happen, we have to look into the empty tomb, said Groat from First Congregational.

He mentioned how Mary Magdalene (John, Chapter 20) discovered the resurrected Jesus when she stayed at the tomb after the others had left. Alone, she wept until she thought she could weep no more. Her best friend and mentor had died, and now, she couldn't even find his body.

"I think when we are alone in our sorrow and feel power-less," Groat said, "is when we become prime pickings for God because we know we can't rely on ourselves."

"The message of Easter is that we can come back from any-thing, that there will be light even in the darkest night," said Pastor Ron Fowler of Arlington Church of God in Akron.

Douglas, the Catholic priest, talked about a recent trip to New York. He visited a fire station in Queens where several of the firefighters were killed when the World Trade Center towers collapsed.

"These were guys who had pulled out the bodies," Douglas said. "They had been to hell and back, but so many of them had such strong faith. They saw evil and death, but chose hope and life instead. That's really the spirit of Easter."

Saturday, March 30, 2002

Ministry Helps the Homeless and Helpless All Year

At the Haven of Rest, there will be Thanksgiving dinner.

And breakfast.

And lunch.

And Haven staffers will serve those meals today, just as they do 365 days a year in Arkon's city mission.

They'll offer food and a place to stay for people like the woman who was found on a corner of Brown Street at 3 a.m. She was sitting, sobbing, on the cold concrete with her four children.

Akron police brought her to the Haven's Harvest Home, a place for women and children. The woman and her children were shivering, scared, dirty and starving.

One of the boys asked for a hot dog. The Haven made the kids a feast of hot dogs, and they almost bit into their frozen fingers as they ate so fast.

Then they were so exhausted, they had to be carried to bed.

The woman's husband had left and she had been evicted from her apartment. She was so frightened, so depressed, so emotionally numb that she couldn't function. The Haven contacted the woman's family, who came to pick her and the children up a few days later.

That's what Thanksgiving is really all about.

It's not about just one day a year when the poor and the homeless appear on television eating turkey and pumpkin pie served to them by once-a-year volunteers.

People who give up a couple of holidays a year for the poor shouldn't be criticized. That's more than most people do. But as the Haven's director, Curt Thomas, said, "We never have problems finding people to help on Thanksgiving and Christmas. It's a different story the other 363 days of the year."

The true meaning of Thanksgiving is found at places like the Haven of Rest, where 800 people will eat 90 turkeys today.

Some of those people will be elderly women who have lost their husbands and are forgotten by their families. They have a place to live. They are almost miserly with their Social Security checks.

But nothing is worse than staring at four walls and a flickering TV set with a phone that never rings on Thanksgiving. It makes you feel you've outlived your life. Most of your family and friends are dead.

Leaving you alone.

At the Haven on this holiday, they will find new friends, smiling faces, warm food and hugs.

They also may find the guy who claimed to be Jesus.

He wandered into the Haven a few weeks ago looking for supper and a bed for the night. The Haven has 100 beds available for men who need a place to stay.

The Jesus guy showed Haven employee Jeff Kaiser where the nail marks and the cut on his side were supposed to be from the crucifixion. The guy's face was scarlet, his eyes nearly bugging out. He almost was hyperventilating as he quoted the Bible.

Kaiser and other Haven employees spent an hour calming the man. He told them he'd been staring at the sun until he nearly went blind "because that's my power source."

Finally, the man grew weary and went to bed. The next day he headed out to the streets.

The Jesus guy is one of the more extreme cases who wander into the Haven. Most of the men and women there are fighting addictions. Most have jobs, usually with temporary agencies.

"My heart goes out to a lot of these guys," Kaiser said. "They get up at 4, 5 a.m., when the vans show up to take them to the temp agencies. They work 10 to 12 hours, then have to walk a mile back to the mission. The dealers know when these guys get back, and they wait for them, trying to get them to take the money they just earned and buy crack."

The dealers are like carnival barkers. So are the prostitutes.

"It's a war for those guys' lives and souls," Kaiser said. "The drugs, the women, the bars, all the temptations. Some of my friends don't understand why I do this work, but it's God's work. And I have seen God change lives that no one believed could be changed."

That brings us to Melvin Fields.

"At least 90 percent of them want to change," said Fields, another member of the Haven's staff. "And some of them do."

The 37-year-old Fields knows.

He was once like them. He started drinking when he was 9 years old. He did drugs for more than 20 years, working most of the time until crack so ruled his life that he took to the streets.

"I lived at the Ocasek parking garage," he said. "I lived in abandoned houses. To this day, I'm amazed when I walk into my apartment, turn on the switch and the light actually goes on."

He lived among the rats, dropping his sleeping bag on a creaky wooden floor surrounded by walls with holes and wires sticking out.

"The shame of living that way gets to you," he said. "You can't believe this is actually happening."

One day, a dealer pulled a sawed-off shotgun on him, and squeezed the trigger.

Click.

The gun jammed.

Fields took off. The dealer jumped in a car, chased him down Akron's mean streets, firing the shotgun, the explosion echoing in Fields's ears as a shot whizzed past his head.

Later that day, Fields went to the Haven for a meal. He heard about the drug and alcohol program at the mission and decided he had nothing left to lose. His life already should have been gone.

Fields spent 29 months living and working at the Haven in the early 1990s before he believed he was ready to find a new life.

And for the last seven years, he has worked with the same street guys as a member of the Haven's staff.

"When I was sober, I was always a good employee," Fields said. "So are these guys. I admit, there are times when I just want to shake them, to tell them what Jesus Christ can do if they only open their hearts. Hey, I was suspicious and in denial when I started. And I was scared. But God pulled me through."

Some people don't want to hear that—the God part.

They say it's good that the Haven has the food, the free beds, the free clothes, the home for battered and lost women and children, and the rehabilitation programs. Even the computer training, the apartment finding and the job placement are great.

But why coat it all in Jesus Christ?

"Because we are a Christian mission and we know God has His hand on this," said Thomas, whose father started the Haven of Rest in a small storefront on North Howard Street. in 1943.

The Haven takes no government money. It has a budget of $4 million a year, and operates debt-free thanks mostly to thousands of small donations each month.

The goal of the mission is more than to feed the hungry and give a bed to the weary. It's to touch their hearts, to give them another way of seeing life.

But some don't like all the prayer and preaching.

There was one middle-aged man who had lost both feet to frostbite and arrived at the mission using two artificial legs to walk. He became so irate during the evening prayer that he stormed out of the dorm into the streets, dragging himself on his hands and stubs of his legs, forgetting even to take his artificial legs. A Haven staff member carried the legs out to him as the man left, cursing God and the mission.

At the Haven, the stories flow with the food and prayers.

There was a woman who was a gambler. She had children with three different men she met at the racetrack. And all three relationships crumbled because of the gambling.

She lost her children, ended up living five years on the streets of Cleveland, spending most of her time in the Tower City mall, eating scraps of food left on the tables in the food court. She never drank, never did drugs, yet never could get a handle on her life.

She eventually was raped, then contracted thyroid cancer and a disease of the pancreas. She spent four months in the hospital before arriving at the Harvest Home this spring.

Now she has her own apartment, gets Social Security disability benefits because of her health problems, and is re-establishing contact with her children. She said she hasn't gambled for seven years.

"If it wasn't for addictions and mental illness, we wouldn't have much to do," said Eileen Thomas. She is the wife of Haven director Curt Thomas and runs the Harvest Home for women on North Prospect Street.

At the Haven, staff members estimate that 80 percent of the people they help have drug or alcohol problems, or both. At least that many come from almost hopeless home situations. Missing fathers. Drugs and booze. No stability. Violence.

It may sound like a bad movie or a story heard so often that no one really listens anymore.

But these lost people are on the street, and they need a place to go.

"The women usually have been abused (sexually or physically) early in life," Eileen Thomas said. "Most have been looking for a man to save them, and they've grabbed onto the wrong guys. The Harvest Home is often the safest place they've ever lived."

The men are angry, hurt, tired and confused.

As the Haven's Ben Walker said, "They have marriage problems, child support problems, addiction problems. It's seldom just one problem."

But today, the Haven of Rest offers a place for these men and women to bring their problems. A place where they can eat good food, hear a little preaching and have a safe place to stay.

And it's there for them not just on Thanksgiving, but every day.

There's Real Meaning Behind Christmas—Once We Put Aside Family Feuds And Shopping Lists

A few weeks ago, I heard this advertisement for a national TV network:

"Tonight at 7: A Charlie Brown Christmas. Charlie Brown laments the materialism of the season. . . . Next up: Who Wants to be a Millionaire?"

Welcome to Christmas, where the messages collide, where Charlie Brown leads off and greed bats cleanup in your TV lineup.

When I was growing up, Christmas often was about family feuds.

It began with my mother, who was always 15 minutes late, and my father, who insisted on being 10 minutes early. My father and I would sit in the car, motor running, my father steaming and stewing, waiting for my mother to finally get ready for church.

When they didn't argue on the way, there was a silence colder than the dead of a December night. Church seldom took the edge off, and I can't remember a single word from a single sermon.

We all have our Christmas stories, and most of them have very little to do with Christmas. Most of us are just so exhausted from all the shopping and preparation, that we just want to *get through it* with some semblance of sanity.

How did it ever come to this, to the point where some people just hate the season because it's so much hassle? Where we end up spending so much time with people whom we'd rather never see again simply because we are related to them?

At Temple, Pastor Mike Mancari's Christmas sermon is: "What's the Big Deal About Christmas?"

"We've made it into such a huge holiday," he said, "that we've lost the meaning."

Which is?

"God so loved the world that He gave His only son, and Jesus can still come into our lives and make a difference," Mancari answered. "I like to think of the Motel 6 commercial, where they always leave the light on. That's how Jesus is with us."

Don't you loathe shopping during this season?

Don't you detest trying to find the right gift for someone who probably will never appreciate it anyway?

Don't you ask yourself, "Why am I doing this?"

Don't you feel your stomach churn as you spend 45 minutes slowly driving around a mall lot, looking for a parking spot and praying some jerk doesn't just back into you?

"Christmas is about giving," said Howard Duma, pastor of Akron Bible Church, "but not the kind of giving that most people do during this season." Duma talked about how his relatively small church on Akron's South Side raised more than $100,000 to put together 3,000 food baskets to deliver to the area's poor.

"We went door to door, handing it to them," he said. "Then we read from Luke, Chapter 2."

That's the same passage, the tale of the birth of Jesus, that Linus recites in "A Charlie Brown Christmas."

"We have a Savior, a living faith, a tangible God that can move into our hearts and change our lives," Duma said. "No matter how much we give, God gave us more. He gave us His best, His son."

This has been a year of death and destruction, of September 11, of thousands dead and thousands more lost, aching and weeping.

"I was watching one of those psychologists on TV who said the people who have buried loved ones wish there was no Christmas because the pain is too great," said the Rev. Paul Schindler of St. Bernard's Catholic Church. "I wondered if that guy was out of his mind."

Schindler talked of his days as a missionary in El Salvador, of nuns being murdered, of tragedy and death being as common as the daily sunrise.

"You get through these times with God, not by ignoring God," he said. "We all have to go on. By ourselves, it's almost impossible."

If the World Trade Center attacks did anything this year, it reminded us that evil is real. Evil is heartless. Evil defies logic.

"It's darkness," said Pastor Knute Larson, of The Chapel. "But Christ came to bring light. He doesn't make us accept the light. He just offers it to anyone who honestly calls out for a Savior."

Larson said without Christ, our motives tend to be selfish, darkness lurks, and sins haunt us. We long for forgiveness, for hope, but we don't know where to look.

The Rev. Jay Groat of Akron's First Congregational Church also talked about light and darkness.

"There are so many people right now in so much pain, some of whom wonder if God is there for them," he said. "Does God care about what they are going through? Can they be forgiven?"

Good questions.

In the darkness, we feel alone. Our suffering is our own, and it seems like it will never end. The problems pile on, and we are weighed down until we are about to be smothered. Think of how it feels when you are about to faint and pass out.

Darkness overwhelms you.

"Jesus is the light of the world," Groat said. "He doesn't

drive all the darkness out of the world, but He is the light. And He can be in us."

Some hear this and say, "You gotta be kidding."

A baby arrives about 2,000 years ago in some neglected corner of Palestine. His mother was a teen-ager, engaged, but still a virgin. She was asked to carry the Son of God by an angel. She agrees, but doesn't quite get it. Her fiance Joseph at first was going to quietly divorce her, but an angel appears to him and tells him to hang in there, so he does.

Jesus then is born to a relatively poor family who couldn't find a place to stay when they traveled to Bethlehem to register for a census and pay taxes. They ended up in a barn because there was no room at the inn.

The Savior came into the world on a bleak, lonely night in a town far away from home. He was born amid the dirt, straw, stench of cows and mules and buzzing of various unsavory bugs.

Among the first visitors were shepherds, who were considered so lowly that they were not allowed to worship inside most temples.

This was all part of God's plan?

Father Joseph Kraker of St. Vincent's Catholic Church thinks so. His message is: "We all can come back to the stable, no matter how dirty we feel or how long we've been away. Just come back."

Pastor Bill Cunningham of Medina's First Baptist Church talked about Jesus' genealogy, how some of the members of the family tree had eaten more than their share of forbidden fruit.

There was King David, the murderer, adulterer, liar—yet considered a "Man after God's own heart." There was Rahab, "a harlot." There was Jacob, who was known as "the deceiver" because he stole his brother's birthright and inheritance.

"None of us are perfect—we all need a savior," Cunningham said. "We all have dark threads woven into our pasts, and we may have some in our future. But what will be our legacy? Are we willing to admit we need to be redeemed?"

Most historians agree there was an actual Jesus. The debate is about his deity. Was he just a man, or was this the son of God?

"It's the question we all face," said The Chapel's Larson. "I talked to a guy who recently gave his life to Christ. For years, he thought Jesus existed—sort of like George Washington. But that it had nothing to do with him today. Jesus has everything to do with today, tomorrow and eternity. He came to rescue us spiritually. That's what this day is all about."

Tuesday, December 25, 2001

This Season, Invite a Shepherd to a Feast

Call someone . . .

Or visit someone . . .

Or talk to someone who is a stranger . . . But make sure it's someone whose phone seldom rings, whose doorbell stays silent, who feels so alone.

That's part of what Christmas is about, reaching out to those who feel untouchable, those who hate this time of year.

Maybe you love Christmas. Maybe it was a great time for your family to get together, for more than presents to be exchanged. Maybe it was about love and traditions and people doing their best to get along.

That's exactly how it should be.

But for too many people, it's a season when families fight, when an uncle drinks too much, an aunt screams too loud, a child sulks, a marriage breaks up in front of your eyes. There are lots of horror stories and horrible memories lurking under some Christmas trees this morning.

That's life.

By the way, that's not to ignore the pain, it's to state a fact: That is life!

Too often, life is messy, petty and unsteady.

Jesus never said, "Hop in my Hummer and ride with me."

He talked about each of us carrying a cross, much as he did. In his first public sermon, he talked about healing broken hearts, helping the blind to see, setting prisoners free.

He didn't promise heaven on earth.

If you really read the accounts of the Christmas story in the New Testament books of Matthew and Luke, you find what House of the Lord Pastor Joey Johnson calls Family Mess.

In his book, *The First Christmas*, Western Michigan University historian Paul Maier believes Joseph was in his middle 20s, Mary was about 16 when they were engaged to be married. Those were the traditional ages, and the marriage was a deal brokered by their parents. The engagement was announced in front of the entire village, a very public event.

The couple were never supposed to be alone until the wedding day. The bride probably had the same dreams of most brides: a husband who cherished and supported her, a secure place to live, children to come. The groom was a carpenter, a small-business man. He probably wanted a wife who loved and respected him, a job that paid the bills, a couple of kids to raise.

Only Mary showed up pregnant with a story about an angel and word from God that she was carrying the Messiah.

Joseph heard that and could have thought two things: "Should I kill her, or just divorce her?"

Under Mosaic Law, he could have her stoned for being unfaithful. But he waited and prayed for a while, then decided to "quietly have her put away," according to the Scriptures. He'd probably divorce her, but try not to embarrass her.

Then Joseph had a dream in which he was told to take care of Mary, that she was indeed chosen by God to bring the Savior into the world. It's hard to imagine that many members of either family swallowed this story. They probably thought Joseph got Mary pregnant and they both were a family scandal.

If his friends did believe Joseph, some may have told him to dump Mary and find a woman who would be loyal to him. They probably told him that it wasn't his duty to care for someone else's child, and even if Joseph did have the dream, who's to say it wasn't really a nightmare?

Put yourself in their places, and suddenly, you realize this couple were very alone, especially because they barely knew each other.

That's also how some people feel this Christmas.

As the baby was about to come, some historians say, the couple traveled from their hometown of Nazareth to Bethlehem, a trip of about 80 miles on foot and/or donkey.

Why?

For a census, used for taxation purposes.

Now there's a noble cause.

Ever wonder how many times a very, very pregnant Mary asked, "Are we there yet?"

Or how many times Joseph asked, "How did I ever get myself into this?"

And both of them asking, "If I'm doing God's will, why is it so hard? Why don't more people help?"

Like when they finally showed up at Bethlehem, found all the hotels were jammed and ended up in a barn for the night. Christmas cards talk about mangers and make them seem like a child's room in an Akron mansion.

It was a barn with stinky animals, stinky straw, stinky rodents, and the couple had to be thinking, "This whole thing just stinks!"

The manger was a feeding trough for animals.

In Jewish culture, the birth of a baby was a grand, public event with all the women gathering to help and watch and encourage the mother. The men were outside with the father, doing what men always have done in these situations—hang around and tell stories.

Mary and Joseph had none of that.

They were alone as the baby was born. They had to be asking themselves, "So this is how the Savior comes? In a barn to a scared couple in a strange town where no one cares about them?"

One of the best parts of the story is the shepherds.

Ever walk into a church and feel like everyone is looking at you, like you don't belong? Ever think the religious people would never accept you? That there's something wrong with you?

That was the shepherds, who were not welcome in most temples for one obvious reason: they were always outside, always with sheep, always in need of a bath.

They smelled.

Yet, they were the first ones summoned by angels to the barn to witness the baby Jesus. They didn't argue about leaving their sheep, or if they were hallucinating, or if what they saw were really angels.

They were so happy someone wanted them to go somewhere, they just went. Maybe that's why God invited them to what became the first party to celebrate the birth of his Son.

And they also were some people who probably weren't worried about stepping into a barn, because the stench of animals was fine to them. They probably didn't even notice it.

There are so many lessons from Christmas. Christians tell you that Jesus came to give us forgiveness for sins, to point us to heaven, to give us hope on earth. God became man to help us have a relationship with our creator.

But even more, God came into the world to say everyone matters to him, especially those who feel rejected and ignored. And God asks us to reach out to them every day, but especially during these days. He wants to use us as his angels to let some shepherds know they are invited to something special, that God does love and care about them.

That's the greatest Christmas gift we can give anyone.

Thursday, December 25, 2003

Fatigued? You're Not Alone: Many of Us Need a Break for Ourselves and for God

Are you tired?

Not tired because someone is deathly ill and you haven't slept for a week.

Just tired, period.

Tired for seemingly no reason. Tired even after a day off. Tired, and you're not even sure why.

You're tired when you drop into bed and ask yourself, "What did I actually accomplish today?"

And you have no answer.

That just makes you even more exhausted.

We've all been there. Some of us live there.

"Most of us are already overworked," said David Loar, pastor of Fairlawn West United Church of Christ, "and we feel guilty when we say no to something."

Or as Rabbi Arthur Lavinsky said, "You know how you get something done? You ask a busy person to do it."

That's true on the job, at school, at church or temple.

Lavinsky said about 15 percent of the people do about 85 percent of the work at his Beth El Congregation in Akron and that percentage is probably true in most situations—religious or business.

Jesus once said, "Bring me your weary, and I will give them rest."

In the Old Testament, Moses went up the mountain to talk to God. The Jews waited for him to come down. Time seemed to stop.

How often does that happen now?

Often, church seems like a call to action. Join this ministry, be a part of that committee, do this, do that.

"We are overprogrammed," said the Rev. Joseph Kraker of St. Vincent Catholic Church in Akron. "People always want to start programs to deal with something, but the same people end up doing all the work."

And it makes them tired.

Most people show up at church or temple exhausted, but some religious leaders don't realize the extent of the stress wearing away at the average person in the pews. They try to inspire, but sometimes it just tires.

Some people stay away from church because it just sounds like more work, which is the last thing they need.

"I think of the experiment with rats in a maze," Kraker said. "The more rats you put in there, the more aggressive and frantic they become. In cities, we are on top of each other, and the pace just seems to get faster and faster."

Loar put it this way: "I wake up to an alarm clock—and alarm is the right word for it."

For many of us, it's like a starter's pistol at the beginning of a marathon. We have appointments. The kids have lessons, games, practices, school. The boss wants calls made, deals closed. There are meals to be cooked, clothes to be washed, rooms to be cleaned.

It's been said that if the devil can't make you sin, he'll make you too busy.

"When I was a kid, we usually ate meals together and went for a drive in the country to get ice cream on Sundays," said Knute Larson, pastor of The Chapel in Akron. "Now, research shows most families eat together only once or twice a week. And who drives anywhere for pleasure? No one seems to have time."

Rabbi David Lipper of Akron's Temple Israel said, "Making it worse, we tend to get overloaded on the negative."

We listen to the news and it sounds like society is going straight to hell—every day! Because our schedules are so tight, the slightest delay threatens to ruin our day. On top of that, it seems the whole world is ready to blow up!

Soon, we're feeling angry, frustrated and overwhelmed.

And often, we're not even sure why.

So what's the answer?

Easy—just *stop*.

No kidding, but who has the time?

The A.C. Nielsen Co. claims the average person watches TV for three hours and 46 minutes per day. That's hard to believe.

Another poll says the average person spends 49 minutes a day on e-mail, and considers most of it worthless. That's the truth.

As Kraker said, "Doesn't it seem like all these labor-saving devices have just made us work harder?"

How often have we said, "If I could just have 15 minutes a day to myself! No phones. No kids. No nothing. Just me."

Even better, just God and me. And time to think and me. And time to pray and me. And time to read and me.

Sometimes, it seems like we schedule time for everything and everyone, but we don't schedule a little time for us, time that we really need.

Loar offered this idea: "One day, I'm going to have one of those big tent revivals. But instead of getting everyone all pumped up, I'm just going to say,—'OK, everybody, just relax.'"

Now that's something we all need.

Saturday, August 31, 2002

Give Up the Guilt and Enjoy Your Family

Ever feel like a little kid?

We may be successful. We may have children. We may have grandchildren. But when we get together with relatives for the holidays, suddenly, we are different people.

We're the little brother or sister. We're the son or daughter who had trouble in high school.

We're the dumb one. The smart one. The clumsy one. The one who was supposed to do better in life.

We're the one who married the wrong person, even though that was 20 years ago and we now have a great spouse.

We're the one who didn't quite measure up, even though we now have a good job, a solid marriage.

We're with our extended family, and we are supposed to walk in the old shoes we thought we threw away years ago.

"We're frozen in time as children in relationships that can't advance," says Pastor Bill Mitchell of Abundant Grace Church in Hartville.

This doesn't happen to everyone in every family. But most of us have experienced it.

When I was an infant, I had colic. For much of my first year, I cried through most nights.

Guess what? I don't remember having colic.

But when I was in my 30s, I'd still hear my father tell relatives about how I kept him and my mother up all night. The only way I'd shut up was if they'd carry me from one end of the house to the other, back and forth, back and forth.

I'd hear that and force a smile.

But down deep, I felt like I was still in diapers.

"It creates an overwhelming sense of inadequacy," Mitchell says.

Pastor Terry Holley of Medina Heartland Church mentions the rejection we experience when our families change. People move. People die. Relatives don't want to see us, except at funerals.

We need to realize that these people should not be that important to us; we can't let their rejection define us.

Ever notice how our deepest wounds come from a mess in the family? Or how the one person hardest to forgive is a family member?

Or how just walking into the house where we grew up instantly changes us? The memories can be good or depressing, but they're always powerful.

Jesus certainly spoke the truth when he said in the New Testament book of Luke: "A prophet is without honor in his hometown."

His relatives and friends continued to see him as a carpenter's son, not as someone who was about to alter history forever—just as some people see us for who we once were, not who we are becoming.

"That happens in a lot of relationships," says pastor Knute Larson of The Chapel in Akron and Green. "We met someone, and that is how we think of them. It also happens with Jesus. Our first exposure forms our opinion, and we never let it grow."

It's easy to fall into this trap.

We can still see our brothers and sisters through the lens of how they treated us when we were young. Pain is often involved.

But sometimes they grow up, shape up and then show up in our lives, and we need to give them the benefit of the doubt.

That doesn't mean putting ourselves at risk if this was once a dangerous person. But in most cases, we should keep an open mind.

I've always thought that's what Jesus meant when he said, "Judge not, lest you be judged" in the seventh chapter of Matthew.

We have to make judgments about people every day: Should we do business with them? Trust them? Help them?

But we should not condemn them. It's God's job to figure out their eternal destiny, not ours.

Some of us feel condemned by our own families. Or we've done that to a relative.

Either way, it's wrong.

And it's why this time of year can be so emotionally draining for so many people.

Saturday, January 3, 2004

It's That Time of Year: What's Worth a Resolution?

We all know about New Year's resolutions.

But for me, the new year's arrival sometimes is tackled by regrets.

Instead of looking ahead, I stare in the rear-view mirror.

What I should have said . . .

What I should have done . . .

What I shouldn't have said or done . . .

I remember some days when the world would have been better off if I had been held hostage, tied up and gagged and not allowed out of the house.

I tell myself that I really want to change. I tell myself that I need to read the Bible more.

Last year, I mentioned that to a friend, and she bought me a Bible that's broken down by day. You can read the Bible in a year. Just keep up with the schedule.

That was in June.

By August, I was a few weeks behind.

By October, I was a few months behind.

By December, I had just quit, figuring I'd start all over and begin in the new year.

Right now, I'm a day behind, unless I make the time to read tonight.

How hard is it to find 15 minutes a day to read?

Why can't I just promise: "This year, I'll find that 15 minutes. This year, I will listen more than I talk. This year, I will not try to impress people by being the expert. This year, I'll try not to be sarcastic."

This year . . .

Why is it that this year I tend to think I'll act like I did last year?

It's probably because I know me too well.

And, sometimes, I just get so tired of me. My problems. My weaknesses. My career. My dreams.

The new year comes and I know I should be thankful. I know God has blessed me outrageously. I know I have nothing to complain about.

But I complain.

Then I complain to myself about my complaining.

I'm not like this all the time—hopefully, not even most of the time.

But sometimes I just get stuck—on me.

Ron Grinker was a respected pro basketball agent who died several years ago. He also was a devout Jew who told a story about 20 people who each wrapped up all their problems in a bag.

"The 20 bags were put in the middle of the floor," he said. "Then everyone was allowed to sort through the bags and pick a bag of problems to be their own."

"What happened?" I asked.

"Everyone claimed their own problems," he said. "At least we know our own problems, even if we don't know how to deal with them."

Ain't that the truth?

I really believe the hardest part of making the new year different is believing we can be different. It's really believing that we are not prisoners to the things we did and the things done to us.

In Chapter 3 of his letter to the Philippians, Paul wrote, "Forgetting what is behind and looking to what is ahead, I press forward to win the prize that God has for me."

Paul wrote this from jail, where he probably had a lot of time to think about what went wrong in his life. He had made a dramatic conversion to Christianity, and certainly became a major figure in that early church. But he also seemed to be somewhat haunted by his past, when he persecuted and perhaps even killed Christians.

Forgetting what is behind . . .

I don't know if we can ever really do that.

What I really resolve to do this year is to forgive myself, to let some things go, to realize I can't change the past.

I can't make everyone like me, or even forgive me. But I can put some of my problems in a bag and just leave it in the middle of the floor, especially if that bag has a bunch of old problems with people and things that are long gone.

And if others want to pick up that bag of problems, they can have it.

Saturday, January 4, 2003

ACKNOWLEDGMENTS

Thanks to Jan Leach, whose idea it was for me to write about issues of faith, and who had the guts to let someone write about God in the newspaper. Jan also edited and picked the columns for this book.

Thanks to David Gray, who is willing to publish a sportswriter's thoughts on faith.

Thanks to Faith Hamlin, a wonderful friend and agent.

Thanks to Mike Needs, whose behind-the-scenes work was very helpful to this book.

Thanks to some pastors and friends who have really helped my spiritual growth: Ron Fowler, Diana Swoope, Joey Johnson, Knute Larson, and Fred and Bunny Perkins.

About the Author

Terry Pluto is a faith and sports columnist for the *Akron Beacon Journal*. He also is the author of 19 books. He has twice been nominated for the Pulitzer Prize for commentary, has twice been named the nation's top sports columnist, and has been named Ohio Sportswriter of the Year eight times. He has also won an Amy award for his faith writing.

He and his wife, Roberta, help lead weekly prison ministry services at Summit County jail; they also volunteer at the Haven of Rest City Mission in Akron.